# PREACH THE WORD

Russell L. Mast

Faith and Life Press
Newton, Kansas

Cover illustration: Detail from an etching by Jan Luyken (1649-1712).
Cover design: by John Hiebert, Mennonite Press.


Library of Congress Catalog Card Number: 68:28782.

Published by Faith and Life Press for the Committee on the Ministry, General Conference Mennonite Church, Newton, Kansas.
Scripture quotations are from the Revised Standard Version of the Bible, copyrighted 1946 and 1952, unless otherwise indicated and are used by permission. Printed in the United States of America.

*To my wife*

*Alma*

Whose companionship has sustained me by her love and whose insight has often sharpened my understanding.

# Foreword

GOOD BOOKS ON PREACHING ARE STILL RARE, ESPECIALLY those which wrestle fruitfully with the theology of proclamation. These chapters by Russell Mast, growing out of years of effective preaching ministry and fertilized through a year of sabbatical study in Scotland, in dialogue with such mentors as James S. Stuart and T. F. Torrance, were first shared with the Pastors' Seminar at Mennonite Biblical Seminary, Elkhart, Indiana, in October 1967. Their strong positive impact as "a word to the situation" evoked directly and vigorously a request for their publication. They appear in print, not because the author asked for this, but because in the judgment of a larger group of persons engaged in preaching ministries, they constitute a significant contribution to the current conversation concerning the continuing role and meaning of preaching in the life and ministry of the church.

In current discussions concerning the nature and value of preaching, two basic errors emerge in a variety of forms. A first error is to expect too much of preaching. This error is to see the sermon as being "the answer" to all of the needs of the congregation as it seeks to fulfill its ministry in the world. In this view, which gained strong impetus through the exaltation of preaching by the Protestant Reformation, it comes to be expected that the pulpit is not only a focal center of church life and ministry, but that all the solutions for personal and corporate problems, or at least most of them, must come from this place. Other functions of congregational life and ministry tend to be minimized or are at least given a secondary place in relation to the pulpit ministry and the one who carries responsibility for this. The man in the pulpit comes to be viewed as a performer. Congregations vie with each other to secure as their pastor "a great preacher," and pride themselves when other people are duly impressed by the weekly performance in the pulpit.

The almost inevitable consequence of this is that when anything goes wrong in the life of the church, or the congregation fails to fulfill its ministry in the world, it is the pulpit which becomes the scapegoat and it is the preacher who is then made "to bear the sins of the whole people." This inflated view of the pulpit and of the preaching ministry has brought great havoc in many congregations. It has made the congregation into "a community of sermon hearers" which sometimes becomes a substitute for "the doing of the Word." It has fed the great temptation of congregations to avoid their proper responsibility to participate in the proclamation of the Word through life and lips. It has tended to create situations of reaction in which preachers have been driven out of their pulpits. It has, therefore, caused thoughtful and dedicated young persons open to Christian ministry to look for other ways than pastoral patterns to express their discipleship to Jesus Christ.

A second basic error is to expect too little of preaching. This is expressed on both popular and sophisticated levels. It is manifest in those who already "expect nothing" when the sermon begins, and who may then on occasion express surprise when they discover that something of significance came to them from God. It is expressed by those who call for a moratorium on preaching, or even the dispensing of "the gathered congregation" altogether. It is propounded by theologians and sociologists who lack understanding and appreciation of a "theology of proclamation." It tends to ignore the biblical mandate which arises from within the gospel itself, the long and distinguished history of preaching through the centuries of God's people, and the possibilities and manifestations of a contemporary renewal of preaching through the Holy Spirit. The Holy Spirit is not limited to the pulpit and to the preaching of sermons but neither is He excluded from this dimension of the church's being.

The contribution of this book serves more of a corrective to the second error than to the first. It grounds preaching solidly in biblical theology and sets it into proper perspectives. It is Christ-centered in its understanding of the gospel which is to be proclaimed and reflects a depth and breadth of theological awareness and contemporary sensitivity which should win for it a wide and thoughtful reading not only by pastors but by others as well. It is hoped that its further impact on those who preach and those who hear preaching will help to make preaching a genuine encounter with Jesus Christ and His Word.

ERLAND WALTNER

Elkhart, Indiana
April 18, 1968

# Preface

WHATEVER IS TO BE SAID IN FAVOR OF PREACHING IN OUR day must be said with the sober realization that much of it will meet with doubt and perhaps even with ridicule. On all sides it is being said that preaching no longer communicates much of anything to the mind of modern man. It leaves him untouched at those points where he must come to grips with the hard realities of life or the massive iniquities of our age. Therefore, he does not want more words; he wants more convincing deeds. He has had enough of sermons and is waiting now to see some decisive action. What evidence is there that all the preaching that has taken place across the centuries has really accomplished anything? Why not change this ancient form of communication for one that is more meaningful or more relevant to the unique problems of our time? Questions such as these become disturbing when one looks seriously at the world and all of its manifest peril.

However, the obligation rests upon the Christian minister to look not only at the world but also at the gospel which is not, first of all, a divine imperative with a moral claim but a divine indicative with a saving offer. It is not only a call to a human activity yet to be accomplished, but it is also the announcement of a divine activity already accomplished. It is only in the realization of what God in Christ has done on man's behalf that the ethical demands of the Christian life can move toward fulfillment. When the minister sees the spiritual antecedents to human behavior and the divine initiative so essential to authentic Christian conduct, then he can begin to feel the compulsion surrounding the church's proclamation. Then he can say with another, ". . . necessity is laid upon me. Woe to me if I do not preach the gospel!" (1 Cor. 9:16).

Ostensibly anything that is said about preaching is addressed primarily to ministers. However, the fact that this should be so is based on several false presuppositions. It is assumed for one thing that to hear the proclamation of the gospel is to be primarily passive, inactive, and uninvolved. As we will have occasion to point out, to hear the Word of God in whatever form it is addressed to man can and ought to be an exacting and demanding experience. Moreover the church's proclamation is the responsibility of the whole church in the proclaiming, hearing, and doing of the Word. Therefore, it is of the greatest importance that all the people of God understand what the preaching of the Word really means. For this reason, the following pages are addressed to the whole church as well as to those who have the special call to preach.

What is presented here is the result of more than tweny-five years in the pastoral preaching ministry, plus a fruitful year of uninterrupted study at the University of Edinburgh in Scotland. This experience helped me to articulate what I have come to feel and believe—never more firmly than now—about the nature of the gospel and its proclamation and about what it means to preach the Word of God to a world of men.

First, it was set down in a series of sermons at the Bethel College Church and presented at the Rocky Mountain Mennonite Conference held at Colorado Springs, Colorado.

The material was then cast into the form of a series of three lectures delivered at the 1967 Pastors' Seminar at the Mennonite Biblical Seminary in Elkhart, Indiana. Chapter 4 was added to what was presented at that time.

For whatever insights may be forthcoming, my indebtedness to those too numerous to name, from whom I have learned more than I can ever say, is humbly acknowledged. My special thanks, however, are extended to the members of the Bethel College Church for releasing me from pastoral duties for a period of ten months and for their patience with me in so many ways; to Dr. Erland Waltner, president of the Mennonite Biblical Seminary, for the encouragement and help he has given to this venture; and to the ministers from the United States and Canada who attended the seminar and made very real to me our common fellowship in the gospel—to all of them I am a debtor.

March 1968

North Newton, Kansas RUSSELL L. MAST

# Contents

The Content of Preaching 1

The Concept of Preaching 19

The Context of Preaching 43

The Consequences of Preaching 65

*"I charge you in the presence of God and of Christ Jesus . . . preach the word, be urgent in season and out of season . . . do the work of an evangelist, fulfil your ministry."*

2 TIMOTHY 4:1-5

# 1

# The Content of Preaching

ENGRAVED ON THE STONE PULPIT OF THE METROPOLITAN Methodist Church in Detroit, and placed where only the speaker can see, are these words: "Preach the Word." They were placed there at the specific direction of the late Merton S. Rice, who so ably and faithfully fulfilled the command of those words. The time came when one of his own sons went away to the seminary to prepare himself for the ministry. The president of the seminary related that about every ten days or two weeks the son would receive a telegram from his father. It was always the same; it never varied, "Dear Son. Preach the Word. God bless you. Dad."

That should be said over and over again to every seminary student, to every theological professor, to every pastor serving a church. Whether the church be suburban, inner city, village, or rural does not alter in any way the central thrust of its obligation to see to it that in one way or another the Word gets preached. ". . . with its preaching," declares P. T. Forsyth, "Christianity stands or falls." When this is done in the authority of the Spirit, according to Emil Brunner, ". . . the most important thing that ever happens on earth takes place."[1] There is, in fact, nothing in all the world to compare with the high privilege and the sober obligation of standing Sunday after Sunday in that most exposed position in all the world, between the Word of God and the world of men, seeking through a careful exposition of the Scriptures to bring about a living encounter between the two.

While it cannot be said that this high ground is no longer taken in the current religious scene, even among some younger theologians, it is no secret that preaching today is the object of rebuke, attack, and even ridicule. Martin E. Marty observed, "Attend a discussion of theological educators talking about improving the ministry. They can talk for a week and not mention preaching." And a seminary professor said, "Heaven save us from becoming a trade school to turn out parish preachers."

We need not go outside the Mennonite church to find similar expressions. The delegates to a recent church conference were told by one of the speakers that the center of the congregation's life and authority is not the preaching of the Word. An article in a Mennonite periodical declared that the congregation can exist without the sermon. And a student Church Workers' Fellowship was told that working on sermons is a waste of time.

What is probably most distressing is that one is led to infer that this current low regard for preaching was the position of the Anabaptists. The fact is that they stressed the importance of the high and holy call to preach over and over again. Pilgram Marbeck, for example, believed that the ". . . proclamation of the Holy Gospel of Christ" is that "through which the church came into being and still does."[2] From the writing of Menno Simons we read this, "The Gospel, the Word of God, preached without admixture in the power of the Spirit is the only right and proper Seed from which truly believing and obedient children of God are born."[3] And Balthasar Hubmaier declared, "Our faith is not built on the church, but on the preached word of God."[4]

This is not to overlook the fact that there is something wrong with current preaching and that much that passes for it is not authentically Christian. But one does not remedy the situation by giving less thought and care to its pursuit. The present plight of preaching cannot be resolved until we reconsider its place in the purpose of God and in the nature of the gospel. However, it must be recognized that doing so will serve as no guarantee of its wider popular appeal. It will, nevertheless, give to preaching the integrity which it so often lacks. This is the thesis I would like to uphold: that the present low regard for preaching reflects in large measure our growing disregard for the gospel. Paul Scherer observes that a whole generation has now grown up which has never heard the gospel, or at best only a *Reader's Digest* version of it![5] If it is true that much that passes for preaching is not preaching, it is also true that much that passes for the gospel is not the gospel.

## Modern Substitutes for the Gospel

Look now at some of the things which currently pass for the gospel which are not the gospel. We might call them modern substitutes which not only obscure the gospel but desensitize the urgency of its proclamation. What are some of the current emphases that help to rob preaching of its essential content and divest it of its basic integrity?

The first is *humanism*. When Jeremiah declares ". . . the way of man is not in himself" (10:23), humanism replies, "The way of man *is* in himself." In the secular world humanism manifests itself as man come of age who has no need for God, because all of his needs can be met in other ways. In the Protestant world it manifests itself as a view of the Christian faith that is centered in man rather than in God. It sees Christianity primarily as a moral ideal, having to do mainly with ethics.

Even where the ethical ideal is seen in the most stringent terms, it is possible that it may be nothing more than discipleship to a pre-resurrection Jesus who is to be followed by a prodigious achievement in human effort. Accordingly, this humanistic tendency views the church as a voluntary association of those, who having passed the moral entrance examination, are pledged to help one another live by the ethical teachings of Jesus.

One hesitates to be critical at this point because there is much here that is good and because the demands of the Christian life do require us to be morally earnest and ethically serious. Yet good as this is, it is not good enough, for the reason that it does not take seriously enough the religious roots of the moral life as well as the divine side of the nature of the church. Under a blanket of religious illiteracy there is a restless Christianity, a Christianity without foundations.[6] So it does not see the difference between an ethic and a gospel with ethical implications, between a moral teacher and a Savior who makes moral demands, between following a pre-resurrection Jesus and being in a post-resurrection Christ. The Christian life is achieved, says Bonhoeffer, "not by dint of effort 'to become like Jesus.' It is achieved only when the form of Jesus Christ itself works upon us in such a manner that it moulds our form in its own likeness. It is Christ who shapes men in conformity with himself."[7]

Another modern substitute for the gospel is *moralism*.

Moralism may not be quite so ready to rely only on human resources; yet at the same time it is less ethically sensitive than humanism. In moralism the Christian ideal is vaguely defined as love or the brotherhood of man or the Golden Rule. It declares naively, "The Sermon on the Mount is enough religion for me." It is made into a magic panacea for the highly complex problems of an atomic age, a neat formula that will render all the tangled intricacies and all the baffling ambiguities of a world in peril, simple and soluble.

Moralism does not understand the profound depth of human sinfulness nor the sublime height of the divine righteousness. It sees the nature of man, his inner capacity to live the Christian ethic in a manner that is too shallow and superficial. In its preoccupation with sins, specific acts of wrong, it fails to deal adequately with sin as an abiding condition of man's life. Man not only commits sin, he is a sinner. His entire nature is a fallen nature. While the divine image with which he was created is not completely obliterated, it is defaced. As Paul viewed his own nature, he was never morbid, nor did he ever allow his selfhood to wither into a cringing cipher. Yet he never denied the fact that "sin dwelleth in me." Even as a redeemed sinner, he was still a sinner.

The other side of the error of moralism is that it does not see the sublime heights of the divine righteousness. It misses entirely the stringent demands so clearly a part of the New Testament ethic. The righteousness for which Jesus called must exceed that of the scribes and Pharisees, who were morally the best people of the day (Mt. 5:20). A conductor, so I am told, wrote on his score, "As loud as possible." A little later on, he wrote, "Still louder." The

Christian ethical demand is like that. It is virtually an impossible ethic.

Therefore, failing to acknowledge the power which sin continually exercises in our natures, as well as the impossible character of the Christian ethical demand, we tend to substitute an easy moralism. We trivialize morality; we strain at gnats and swallow camels; and we treat trifles as though they were serious matters and serious matters as though they were trifles. The way out of shallow moralism must resist the tendency to become picayune and petty without becoming licentious or lax.

Still another modern substitute for the gospel is *subjectivism*. Here it is not so much a matter of the human resources available to meet the ethical demands, but of personal feelings, experiences, and expressions of the Christian faith. The issue is not so much on how the Christian ideal is to be achieved but on what the Christian faith essentially is. To begin with, subjectivism looks within, to what is deeply felt and genuinely experienced.

At one level subjectivism can verge into a self-centered sentimentalism. There is a type of religious song which reflects almost exclusively the feelings which man has in his Christian experience: "There is sunshine in my soul today." Over against that is the kind of hymn that stresses the objective content of faith: "A mighty fortress is our God." At another level, subjectivism is the very necessary response that we must surely make in our Christian experience. It is a personal awareness and sensitivity that we have of what is given in our faith. Until it is experienced by man in the depth of his being, it cannot be real to him. But when it is, it will move him to very deep feelings. Important as all of these personal feelings, experiences, and expressions are, however, they are the accompaniments of the gospel and not a part of its essence.

In order to understand the meaning of the Christian faith, we must therefore move from our subjective experience to the objective fact behind it. For the essence of the Christian faith is its objective content, not man's subjective experience of it. If we are true to what the proclamation of the church was meant in the mind of God to be, then the essential content of what we proclaim is not our own feelings about religion or even our experiences of God, and certainly not our expressions of virtue. All of these have a very important place in the life of faith, but they do not constitute the essence of the gospel or the content of our preaching. As Paul put it, "We preach not ourselves."

There is a final modern substitute for the gospel to be mentioned. It is *faddism*. This is probably more exclusively a modern phenomenon although Paul may have referred to something like this when he spoke of those who are "tossed to and fro and carried about with every wind of doctrine" (Eph. 4:14). In any case, that is a very apt description of what is currently happening in certain quarters within the Protestant world, and even in the smaller Mennonite world where its influence is more obvious. Never in my own memory has there been such an emphasis on the need for change in the life and practice of the church, such a straining after what is current and new, and such a wholesale rejection of anything that smacks of tradition. An idea or practice is judged by whether it is *in* or *out* rather than whether it is *right* or *wrong*. It is judged by its evidence of change rather than by its faithfulness to the gospel.

Whenever we choose to live in radical discontinuity with

the past, we become what Elton Trueblood calls "an orphan generation." An orphan generation, he goes on to say, is afflicted by the "disease of contemporaneity." "So we cut ourselves off from the wisdom of the ages, including the Bible, because we are too much impressed with changes that may only be superficial." As an orphan generation we are rootless and without foundations and completely deaf to all that the centuries are saying to the hours.

The gospel does, in fact, call for changes, both inside and outside the church. There is no need for me to document that. But that is not the same as saying that change is the gospel. There are, as everyone knows, changes that can prove to be disastrous. The changes that issue from the gospel can save us, but let it be clearly understood that it is the gospel and not the change that does the saving!

## The Rediscovery of the Gospel

Our incipient humanism, our shallow moralism, our ingrown subjectivism, and our ardent faddism give us a disregard for the gospel and a low regard for its proclamation. We will not restore preaching to its rightful place in the life of the church until we rediscover that gospel for which there is no substitute. In place of a self-sufficient humanism, there is a God-appointed revelation. Instead of a shallow moralism, we need a renewed vision of man's peril and God's demand. Behind the subjective nature of man's experience, we need to discover the objective character of God's mighty acts. And finally, we should be guided less by the contemporaneity of the world than by God's disclosure of himself in His Word.

It is not at all difficult to be enamored by all of these modern substitutes for the gospel. Yet they do divert our attention for the gospel which saves. There is a story that in his first painting of the *Last Supper,* Leonardo da Vinci put such a wealth of detail into two cups standing on the table that a friend stared at them in openmouthed amazement. Immediately the artist seized the brush and painted them out of the picture. "Not that!" he shouted. "That isn't what I want you to see! It's the *face*. Look at the *face*." When we recover the centrality of the glory of God in the face of Jesus Christ, we recover the gospel that saves. When we recover the gospel that saves, we recover the content of preaching. And when we recover the content of preaching, we recover its integrity and its indispensability.

It is at this point that I find myself critical of the church renewal movement. It is not that the church does not need renewal. And it is not that the church may not need to reconsider or even alter its structures, forms, or techniques. I would certainly encourage experimentation with new forms of ministry. But let it be abundantly clear: This will not renew the church! Jared Rardin of First Methodist Church at Germantown, who is a part of an experience of renewal in that church, said, "Most of us would be quick to acknowledge that renewal is as much a gift of the original Gift which inspires it, but we turn right back to the moving about of our structural furniture or vigorous efforts to 'create koinonia.' Indeed in our haste to replace the old structures we often end up making golden calves of our new (or wish-dreamed) ones."[8] In my own reading of church renewal literature, I found a persistent emphasis of form over content, structure over spirit, strategy over sainthood, and novelty over authenticity.

Soberly I put it to you; the church will not renew itself sufficiently to be authentically the church in the world simply by tinkering with its structure, or by the invention of clever gimmicks, or by taking its *shape* from the world. All of this may need to be done in the course of time. But surface changes alone never have and never will renew the church. If history has anything to say to us, it is clear that whenever the church has renewed itself, it has done so by going back to the fountainhead of its life and power: God's Word addressed to the world of men that called the church into being. "It can never be the source of its own renewal," says Karl Barth. "Jesus Christ the Lord, is the hope of the church."[9]

In order, then, that the church may return to the source of its renewal, perform its mission in the world and, among other things, be the agent of change in society, I propose that we give special attention to the content of the church's proclamation. For God is a God who speaks and acts; He acts in His speaking and He speaks in His acting. The Word of God comes to us in God's disclosure of himself in Jesus Christ. When Paul wrote to Timothy, he gave it this formulation: "For there is one God, and there is one mediator between God and men, the man Christ Jesus" (1 Tim. 2:6).

## The Word - Event of the Gospel

We are ready to come now to that most important part of our consideration as we try to speak in more detail concerning this Word which God has addressed to man, this gospel that is the power of God unto salvation in the life of man, which is first, last, and always the content of the church's proclamation.

The Word which God addressed to the world of men is, first of all, an *incarnate Word*. "And the word became flesh and dwelt among us." So the Word of God came to life; it assumed bodily, human form. At a point in time and space it entered into the stream of history. This is God's Word incarnate. This is the Man Christ Jesus; this is the revelation, the unveiling, the disclosure of the Word of God to the world of men. It is the story of log cabin to White House in reverse. Paul says that, coming from the very being of God, He "emptied himself, taking the form of a servant, being born in the likness of men" (Phil. 2:7).

That Jesus was a human creature, that He entered fully into the life of man, that He felt the pains, the perils, and the temptations of man, is to make a very important statement about Jesus. It is to say what the New Testament says over and over again. Against the background of the Docetic heresy, which denied that Jesus had a human body and was in any sense a creature of this earth, most of the New Testament was written. So John says, ". . . every spirit which confesses that Jesus Christ has come in the flesh is of God" (1 Jn. 4:2). The writer of Hebrews is even more pointed in his statement of the importance of the humanity of Jesus for His ministry to the life of man: "Therefore he had to be made like his brethren in every respect, so that he might become a merciful and faithful high priest in the service of God . . . For because he himself has suffered and been tempted, he is able to help those who are tempted" (Heb. 2:17, 18).

What we have, then, is a genuine historical event. Something did occur in the stream of history which was nothing less than God's self-disclosure in His Word. His Word is not just a sound ringing through the heavens, or an abstract truth illuminating the mind of man, or a propositional statement. The revelation of His Word is not a truth uttered but a deed done. For in His Word, God took it upon himself to make himself known in Jesus Christ. Emil Brunner summarizes the solid fact on which the Christian faith rests in his statement, "Faith in Jesus Christ is not an interpretation of the world, but it is participation in an event: in something which has happened, which is happening, and which is going to happen."[10] Now we focus our attention on the fact that this has to do with something that has happened.

"In many and various ways God spoke of old to our fathers by the prophets;" said the writer to the Hebrews, "but in these last days he has spoken to us by a Son . . . He reflects the glory of God and bears the very stamp of his nature" (1:1-3). God's Word is therefore supremely a revealing event in which at last the veil of mystery was pulled from the face of God, and Jesus could say of himself, "He that hath seen me hath seen the Father." It is not a Christ-idea, but the very Word of God incarnate which is the fundamental fact of our faith.

The Word which God addressed to the world is also the *eternal Word*. This is of the utmost importance to us, for the only possible way for us to see this revealing event is from the resurrection side. In fact, were it not for the resurrection, we would not be seeing it at all. No one ever stated this in more positive terms and to an audience that was more inclined to be skeptical or even hostile than Peter when he addressed the people in Jerusalem. Here in the same city the tragic events leading up to the crucifixion had taken place. Here even Peter had denied Jesus. And here Jesus had been tried by Pilate, condemned by the people, and crucified by the Roman soldiers. Many of the same people to whom Peter was now speaking had been witnesses to all of these happenings. In fact, he boldly reminded them of their own part in them. But then he moved to this mighty climax: "This Jesus God raised up, and of that we all are witnesses" (Acts 2:32).

In John Masefield's play, *The Trial of Jesus*, there is a conversation between the Roman officer and the wife of Pontius Pilate. It is after the crucifixion and they are thinking of all that had happened in and around Jerusalem. Then they begin to reflect on the kind of person Jesus had been. At one point the Roman officer observes: "If a man believes anything up to the point of dying on a cross for it, he will find others to believe it." A little later the wife of Pilate asks, "Do you think he is dead?" The officer says, "No, lady, I don't." "Then where is he?" she asks. "Let loose in the world, lady, where neither Roman nor Jew can stop his truth."[11]

All of this Peter and the other apostles believed. To them, however, it was not only that a benevolent but deathless influence had now permeated the whole of man's existence. It was rather that this Jesus whom they had known as a teacher in Galilee, a healer of diseases, and a friend of sinners, God had raised up. To them this was more than "The soul's invincible surmise." It was a fact concerning which they were witnesses. There was nothing in the character of those disciples before the resurrection which could explain what they were eventually able to do. For they were terrified and fearful men, hiding behind closed doors, meeting in upper rooms, and walking through back streets. They were smitten with fear, filled with despair, and beset with confusion. But it was the resurrection that put hope into the hearts of hopeless men, that sustained them with courage to face a pagan and hostile world, and that gave them good news to tell wherever they went.

So the incarnate Word is also the eternal Word. He who was fully and completely human, who shared the common lot of man, who felt man's pains and perils and temptations, and who tasted death in its fullest and bitterest was the Man Christ Jesus. This means that he was the Messiah, the anointed one, the one whom God sent into the world, the one whose coming was awaited through the long sweep of Old Testament history, the eternal Word. "The grass withers, the flower fades; but the word of our God will stand for ever" (Is. 40:8).

The Word which God addressed to the world is also the *living Word*. So the two men in "dazzling apparel" said to the friends of Jesus on the resurrection morning, "Why do you seek the living among the dead?" For He was and is the living Christ. The Book of Acts, in a very simple statement, lifts up the decisive fact which convinced the friends of Jesus that the incarnate Christ was also the eternal Christ. In the ninth chapter we read, "He presented himself alive after his passion." And Paul answers from his own experience by saying, "He appeared also to me." Whenever he was in a position of having to defend his apostleship against those who were minded to challenge it, he insisted that Christ was as much alive for him as He was for them, and that the fact of the resurrection had come within the orbit of his own experience quite as much as it had within theirs.

R. W. Dale was in his day a recognized theologian and a scholar of the first order. He was also a great preacher and the minister of Carr's Lane Congregational Church of Birmingham, England. In the midst of an already fruitful ministry there came a decisive turning point prompted by a new awareness of the truth and presence of Christ. In his diary he wrote:

"Christ is alive," I said to myself. "Alive!" And then I paused: "Alive!" And then I paused again: "Alive!" Can that really be true? Living as really as I myself am? . . . I got up and walked about repeating, "Christ is living! Christ is living!" . . . I thought that all along I had believed it; but not until that moment did I feel sure about it. I then said, "My people shall know it. I shall preach it again and again until they believe it as I do now."[12]

The Word of God is unfailingly, everlastingly, and inescapably a living Word. For the Word that was made flesh and dwelt among us is alive forevermore. As Emil Brunner reminds us again: "Faith in Jesus Christ is a participation in an event . . . in something which is happening." For indeed the same Christ who showed himself alive to the early friends of Jesus, to Paul on the road to Damascus, and to Dale at Birmingham, can show himself alive to us. He is not a loving memory but a living presence.

The Word which God addresses to the world is, finally, a *continuing Word*. The Man Christ Jesus, who has been a living presence and who has presented himself alive, has, by virtue of the same fact, made himself available alike to all the generations of men. When in John's Gospel we read, "But as many as received him, to them gave he power to become the sons of God . . ." he was not only describing something that had happened or that was happening, but something that was going to happen as long as time would last. So this promise is just as meaningful today as it ever was. For the Man Christ Jesus "is the same yesterday and today and for ever" (Heb. 13:8). What Jesus was as a friend of sinners and as a giver of life in the body of His flesh, He is today as the living Christ in the person of the Holy Spirit.

"I have yet many things to say to you," said Jesus to His disciples, "but you cannot bear them now. When the Spirit of truth comes (the Holy Spirit, whom I will send in my name), he will guide you into all the truth . . . whatever he hears he will speak, and he will declare to you . . ." (Jn. 16:12f.). So the living Word is the same Word which is also the continuing Word, for the same God who spoke continues to speak. The Christ who presented himself alive is assuredly the same Christ who is available still. And with those who will receive Him, He enters into a genuine encounter, a meaningful relationship. In such a relationship there is both calling and answering, both honest speaking and patient listening, as "deep calls unto deep."

There is a phrase that occurs more than 164 times in all of Paul's letters. Its frequency and simplicity tend to obscure the fact from us that this term is not used in the Synoptic Gospels and could never have been used about any person other than Jesus. It is the phrase, "in Christ," which has a very close relation to a similar term, "in the Spirit," about which we have just been speaking. "Therefore," Paul says, "if any one is in Christ, he is a new creation"—"a new being," as Goodspeed translates it (2 Cor. 5:17). This is the relationship: to have our very being in Him! But at the same time we are in the world, and we have no right or cause to seek to escape it. This means that the Christian life is lived in a state of tension between being-in-the-world and being-in-Christ. So again the Word of God enters the world of men.

We have been speaking about the Word of God—God

acting in His speaking, and God speaking in His acting. This Word is an incarnate, eternal, living, continuing Word, which through the Holy Spirit is as active today as it ever was. In a world desperate in its peril and sick unto death, it is not the contemporaneity of the world but God's disclosure of himself in His Word that will save us. This is our faith; this is our hope. So preach the Word!

## FOOTNOTES

1. Emil Brunner, *Revelation and Reason* (Philadelphia: The Westminster Press, 1946), p. 142.
2. Quoted by Walter Klaassen, *Concern,* No. 9 (1961), 30.
3. J. C. Wenger, ed., *The Complete Writings of Menno Simons* (Scottdale: Herald Press, 1956), p. 164.
4. Quoted by Walter Klaassen, *Word, Spirit and Scripture in Early Anabaptist Thought* (Typewritten Oxford dissertation, 1960, copy in Bethel College Historical Library), p. 71.
5. Paul Scherer, *The Word God Sent* (New York: Harper and Row, 1965), p. 5.
6. T. O. Wedel, *Christianity of Main Street* (New York: The Macmillan Company, 1950), pp. 2-4.
7. Dietrich Bonhoeffer, *Ethics* (London: Collins, The Fontana Library, 1964), p. 80.
8. Stephen C. Rose, ed., *Who's Killing the Church?* "Sainthood Before Strategy," Jared J. Rardin (Chicago: *Renewal* magazine, 1966), p. 71.
9. Karl Barth, *God Here and Now* (London: Routledge and Kegan Paul, 1964), p. 76.
10. Emil Brunner, *Man in Revolt* (New York: Charles Scribner's Sons, 1939), p. 494.
11. John Masefield, *The Trial of Jesus* (New York: The Macmillan Company, 1925), p. 111.
12. A. W. Dale, *Life of R. W. Dale of Birmingham* (London: Hodder and Stoughton, 1898), p. 642.

# 2

# The Concept of Preaching

ALEXANDER WHYTE DESCRIBES SOMEWHERE THE SATURDAY walks which he had with Marcus Dods in and around Edinburgh at the turn of the century. Whyte was the pastor of what was then called Free St. George's Church, and Dods was professor of New Testament and Principal of New College, now a part of the University of Edinburgh. "Whatever we started off with in our conversations," Whyte recalls, "we soon made across country, somehow, to Jesus of Nazareth, to His death, and His resurrection, and His indwelling."

In the last chapter, we ventured the statement that much that passes for the gospel is not the gospel, even as much that passes for preaching is not preaching in any authentically Christian sense. The picture of these two men walking together in conversation portrays for us, in terms that are vivid and compelling, what the gospel is and what true preaching is. So whenever you start in your text or theme, you should somehow make your way across "to Jesus of Nazareth, to His death, and His resurrection, and His indwelling." For the gospel is Jesus Christ, whom to proclaim is true preaching. This is the content of preaching: the Word of God to the world of men, which, we said, is an incarnate, eternal, living, and continuing Word. Out of this essential content of preaching we must formulate our concept of preaching. To this task we now give our attention.

There is, however, something more that is portrayed to us in this remembrance of long ago to which we have just made reference. It points at once to the necessary precondition of an adequate concept of preaching and to the reason why, particularly in America, that adequate concept has not always presented itself. Is there not something significant in the fact that a great theologian and Bible scholar should walk alongside of, and enter into a deep conversation with one who was a great pastor and preacher? I think there is. For it points up the kind of dialogue that is so crucial and necessary between theology and preaching. Not only does preaching need to be informed by the insights of theology; it needs to have a theological understanding of its task. We can say, on the other hand, not only does theology need to take preaching into its primary consideration, but it needs to find in preaching its very life.

Emil Brunner, who through the years of his theological productivity kept up a weekly preaching assignment, confessed, "Again and again I have seen that decisive theological ideas have come to me while preparing a sermon, and on the other hand how the depth of my sermon has been conditioned by my theological work." But he goes even beyond that, "Scholarly work in theological and philosophical areas was and still is strictly subordinated to the proclamation of the gospel . . . I was and still am above all a preacher of the Good News."[1]

Karl Barth, whose weekly preaching assignment was in the city jail, declared, "There is an unavoidable affinity between preaching and theology. Theology cannot and should not be ashamed of this affinity."[2] Lest there be any who were not properly vaccinated against the disease of "contemporaneity" in the last chapter and are developing certain noticeable symptoms by saying, "But Brunner and Barth are now of another generation," let me quote the brilliant young successor to Barth, Heinrich Otto. In his first major book, *Theology and Preaching,* he writes, "In order to be able to preach one must engage in dogmatic reflection. While the dogmatic theologian in order to teach dogma must constantly bear in mind the mission of preaching."

The situation in America is less conducive to the kind of synthesis of which these European theologians are such eloquent examples. There is a gap which is growing wider between the preacher and the theologian, between the pastor and the scholar, and between the seminary and the church. That the overburdened pastor is often theologically impoverished and the theologically trained scholar is often pastorally inexperienced takes its toll at one point in particular. Neither the pastor-preacher nor the scholar-theologian ever get around to hammering out a thoroughgoing theology of preaching. P. T. Forsyth did it sixty years ago in his *Positive Preaching and the Modern Mind,* which is still one of the best books on the subject. Karl Barth did it in the relevant passages of the *Church Dogmatics* as well as in his shorter writings. Dietrich Ritschl did it most recently in *A Theology of Proclamation.* Others have done it and many more need to do it. What is often said carelessly about preaching reveals the theological vacuum in which so much thinking about it is carried on.

To come to an adequate theology of preaching which ought to be the legacy of every seminary graduate as he goes out to serve a church requires more than a course or two in homiletics which does little more than deal with a few techniques of communication. This is not to belittle the importance of learning how to preach or to minimize the importance of the preparation and delivery of sermons. Anything less than the very best that we can do is an impertinence and a mockery. This is only to say that one is not likely to learn how to preach without a theological understanding of what preaching is. For thus understood, preaching is not a mere technique of communication. The Christian preacher is not the successor of the Greek orator such as Cicero, but of the Hebrew prophet such as Isaiah. The orator comes with an inspiration, the prophet with a revelation.[3] So preaching is not bound by Ciceronian rhetoric, "to teach, to please, to persuade," nor is it to be measured by how well it succeeds in producing the usual results of good rhetoric. Conrad Harry Massa states the matter with bold accuracy: "Preaching does not fail to be valid Christian preaching by failing to persuade or edify; it fails to be valid Christian preaching by failing to be a true confrontation of men by God through the person of the preacher."[4]

To understand preaching theologically, we are saying, we must allow the concept of preaching to grow out of its content. That content is the Word of God to the world of men—God speaking in His acting, God acting in His speaking. In a very moving passage, Professor Stewart summarizes it, "Enshrined at the heart of the faith are facts of such perennial vitality and incalculable force that you will never, to your dying day, tell more than a fraction of the truth that God has blazed across your sky . . . Is not its wonder as fresh and unspoilt still as when the morning stars sang together and the sons of God shouted for joy?

And are God's mighty acts in history and redemption less enthralling than His mighty acts in nature . . . ? Therefore settle it with your own souls now that, whatever else you may do or leave undone, you will preach in season and out of season God's redemptive deed in Christ."[5]

Here is the point at which the content of preaching forms itself inescapably into a concept of preaching. For the moment we understand what it is we preach; we will soon understand what preaching is. When we really hear the Word, we will begin to grasp what it is to preach the Word. Let us now detail the concept under four major headings.

## Preaching as Proclamation

First of all, preaching the Word has the character of a proclamation. Behind the word *proclamation* is the Greek, *kerygma*. This is the characteristic New Testament word which refers to the essential Christian message, the good news of the gospel with which the apostles went out to confront a pagan world. We spoke about it as the Word of God to the world of men. It is God speaking in His acting; His acting in His speaking. So the *kerygma* is the enthusiastic recital of the mighty acts of God culminating in the mightiest of all His mighty acts—His self-disclosure in Jesus Christ, the Word made flesh. So great was this mighty act that theologians speak of it not improperly as an event. As the writer of the Epistle to the Hebrews reminds us, ". . . the world was created by the word of God" (Heb. 11:3). The word-event of redemption is not unlike the word-event of creation in its enormity and significance. The word-event of redemption—the incarnate, eternal, living, continuing word—is nothing other than the apostolic *kerygma.*

As we try now to think through the proclamatory nature of Christian preaching, notice first of all its public character. The apostolic message was the *kerygma,* but the proclaimer of the message was the *keryx,* or the herald. He was like the town crier of olden days with a public announcement or declaration to deliver for the king or ruler to the entire village. He even has some affinities with Paul Revere, riding through the streets shouting, "The British are coming! The British are coming!" Only the apostolic *kerygma* was not a message of doom but of deliverance. It has urgency, but it was the urgency of "good news." It was like the disciples running back from Emmaus to Jerusalem to proclaim the resurrection fact.

That there is a place for an intimate, private conversation between two people, even as Jesus spoke with Nicodemus, no one will deny. But we lose something of the essential nature of the *kerygma* when we disregard its public character. Precisely "because it is public, connected with community," says Brunner, "it is the primary form of Divine Revelation."[6] Indeed the "conversational style" of preaching fails also to capture this important dimension of the apostolic proclamation. W. E. Sangster, late minister of Central Hall in London, has some telling sentences about those who like "a little intimate chat between you and me." Aside from the fact that most people are unable to hear such a chat in a congregation even of average size, Sangster reminds us that a herald does not have an intimate chat with anyone, but proclaims a message from his king.[7]

Concerning the proclamatory nature of Christian preaching, notice now its personal character. One of the classic definitions of preaching is the one by Phillips Brooks. "Preaching is the communication of truth by men to men. It has two essential elements, truth and personality."[8] This understanding which he developed as long ago as 1877 is interesting since he seems to have antedated so much that has been written since 1923, the year that Buber published his book, *I and Thou*. It is now commonplace among theologians to say with Brunner, "God's personal approach to men and women is always through other persons."[9] H. H. Farmer does, in fact, see preaching as a personal encounter of the I—Thou variety.[10] We will come back to this again when we speak of the context of preaching, but let it be said here that it is quite possible for preaching to be carried on in a true dialogic relationship, even as it is possible for a discussion group to be nothing more than a series of monologues!

The herald as he proclaimed the message of his sovereign was a person addressing other persons, a fact which always belonged to the essential nature of the apostolic *kerygma*. It was not a loud noise echoing from one end of the village to another or the wild shriek of an ambulance racing down the street. It was one person saying to another person in urgent entreaty, "Be reconciled to God." For verily God is making His appeal through one man to another (2 Cor. 5:20). So the personal character of Christian preaching becomes evident when that which is proclaimed by one person is brought to focus on the life of another. Preaching, one may observe, goes awry more often at this point than at any other. Often it is like sheet lightning—concerning itself with lofty ideals, magnificent truths, abiding principles. It is certain that all this fills the sky with a bright heavenly glow. Yet for all that, such preaching never strikes anywhere! It ought to be like forked lightning, blazing its way to a point of impact and then striking, as once the prophet Nathan said to David, "Thou art the man."

Charles Clayton Morrison was always a keen and perceptive observer of preachers and their preaching. With characteristic insight he wrote about what he called "the public privacy of the pulpit." He went on to say that it is as though an invisible private wire ran from the preacher to the listener so that he was able to hear and respond to that which was meant for him alone. As a servant of the Word, the minister stands in a unique relation to that which is deepest in the life of man. He feels the judgment, the rebuke, the comfort, or the guidance as need may require. Then—it may be unknown to the minister or the other worshipers—he makes his response to God. There are things that need to be shared with fellow Christians, but there are also confidences and things private with a man's soul and his God.

We are living "between the times." Our present dispensation of time is tucked snugly between the first and the final coming of Jesus. The stage on which our present drama of history is enacted is the very place where our present age overlaps the age to come. For the firstfruits of that coming age have already appeared in Jesus' first coming. To live, therefore, is to be keenly aware of the true character and signficance of the present moment and to see it in the light of the past and the future. "It is the holding of past and future in the 'now' of faith."[11] Yet we live out our days in preoccupied indifference, moving about in a cloud of unknowing, allowing precious moments to slip down the drain never to be recovered.

The proclamation of the church in the event of Christian

preaching has an urgency about it because it has to do with the present moment, the living "now." It presses for an immediate response. It calls for a verdict. It demands an answer. "Jesus came into Galilee, preaching the gospel of God, and saying 'The time is fulfilled, and the kingdom of God is at hand; repent, and believe in the gospel' " (Mk. 1:14). Religion in our day has become a much-discussed subject. Aided by a plethora of popular books stressing the unusual, the unconventional, and even the bizarre in religious thought, religion does get talked about and discussed.

Yet there is always an important difference between a discussion of religion and the proclamation of the gospel. For proclamation has a present, immediate, urgent character about it. In the present moment, the here and now, it calls for an immediate verdict, an emphatic answer, a conscious decision. When, therefore, the Christian proclamation is addressed audibly as well as personally, it brings it out of the past; it raises it from a mere dead letter; it quickens it with new life. Thus coming forth out of the tomb of an ancient record, it does in the very process of proclamation confront man with a personal summons to his own soul. It lays upon the human heart an immediate demand for faith. ". . . what shall I do with Jesus who is called Christ?" (Mt. 27:22). "Behold, now is the acceptable time; behold, now is the day of salvation" (2 Cor. 6:2).

### The Witness of Scripture

In the second place, preaching the word is informed by the witness of Scripture. The Bible has a unique and decisive relation to the apostolic *kerygma* and the preaching of the Word. Oddly enough, that part of the Bible which speaks most directly to that relationship is relegated to a mere parenthetical expression, which, in some translations, is even enclosed within parentheses. The statement has the further handicap of a long history of misinterpretation and misuse. This is all the more unfortunate in view of the fact that it is meant to convey a profoundly important insight. Jesus is in the midst of a lengthy controversy with the Jewish leaders, in which He is trying to explain who He is, what is His relation to God and what, above all else, He seeks to do in the lives of men. Then He turns to them and addresses them directly: "You search the scriptures, because you think that in them you have eternal life; and it is they that bear witness of me; yet you refuse to come to me that you may have life" (Jn. 5:39).

There are three things to note very briefly about this passage. First of all, this is not meant primarily as an exhortation to search the Scriptures as the King James translation seemed to indicate. As a matter of fact, Jesus is rebuking the Jewish leaders for doing that very thing, as though eternal life could somehow burst forth from the ink, the paper, or the shape of the letters. The second thing Jesus is saying is that it is He who gives life eternal, not the letter of Scripture. So He rebukes them for not coming to the source of life. And yet, far from rejecting the Scriptures, He actually emphasizes their very crucial significance by saying, ". . . it is they that bear witness to me." So Luke records the fact that when, after the resurrection, Jesus overtook two of His disciples on the road to Emmaus, ". . . he interpreted to them in all the scriptures the things concerning himself" (24:27).

The Scriptures, therefore, constitute the original witness

of the Word. Whenever Jesus referred to the Scriptures as bearing witness to himself, He was, of course, thinking of the Old Testament. We take it for granted that this is plainly true of the New Testament, but it is also true, as Jesus would have us understand, of the Old Testament as well. At the heart of biblical faith is the affirmation that God acts in history, that history is His Story, that the stream in which He works out His redemptive purpose begins with the call of Israel and culminates in the Man Christ Jesus. It is to this that the Scriptures bear a written witness, in both Old Testament and New.

But the Scriptures as the witness of the Word are the original witness. That is to say, it is a careful and faithful recording of what men saw concerning the mighty acts of God, which is what the word *witness* really means. So Luke in the preface to his Gospel says, "Inasmuch as many have undertaken to compile a narrative of the things which have been accomplished among us, just as they were delivered to us by those who from the beginning were eyewitnesses and ministers of the word, it seemed good to me also, having followed all things closely for some time past, to write an orderly account for you . . ." (1:1-3). We are saying that these accounts are original witnesses to the Word. They constitute the primary written sources of our faith. They cannot be replaced, and for them there are no substitutes. Their place and position are utterly unique.

But the Scriptures also constitute a remembered witness of the Word. We cannot say it often enough that Jesus is not a loving memory but a living presence, available to anyone who is prepared to open his life to Him and live in Him. For the Christian faith is a participation in something that *is* happening. But to know precisely what is happening, to know what the living presence of Christ is like, we will need to know what has happened; we will need to know all we can about the historic Jesus and all that led up to and away from His coming in the flesh. We will need to know precisely what Jesus did, how He lived, what He said. And we will need to study, understand, and know those facts so deeply imbedded in man's history and in his humanity to which the Bible is a remembered witness.

History is written because some things of great importance deserve to be remembered; and man so readily forgets what he needs to remember and even wants to remember. Jesus assured us of His continuing presence when He promised, "Lo, I am with you always." But He also wanted men to remember carefully and concretely who He was and what He was like when He commanded, "Do this in remembrance of me." The apostles went forth to proclaim a risen Christ who was also a living Christ and an available Christ. But they also took the time and energy to commit to writing the historic roots of the faith that was in them. So the faithful servant of the Word can say in our day as when the church was yet in its infancy, "That which was from the beginning, which we have heard, which we have seen with our eyes, which we have looked upon and touched with our hands, concerning the word of life . . . we proclaim also to you" (1 Jn. 1:1-3). So it is a remembered witness that attests to past revelation, to all that God has done, and to His Word incarnate in Jesus Christ.

Once again the Scriptures constitute a permanent witness of the Word. We have said that the Word is a continuing word, addressing itself with newness and freshness as life turns unexpected corners and men encounter unprecedented situations. But how do we resist the temptation to read into the guidance of the Word what we ourselves wish to find there? What antidote is there for the "Peril of Modernizing Jesus"?[12] These are questions that we need to face, for we are so eager to make Jesus the champion of our causes, so sure that our methods were really His methods, and our way of working just like His. So we fall into the habit of saying, "Jesus taught . . ." or "Jesus said . . ." or "Jesus did. . . ." Then we follow by giving some general statement of our own which may have nothing to do with what Jesus actually taught or said or did.

While Jesus is "Our Eternal Contemporary,"[13] as one theologian put it, and while Jesus does address himself to the changing conditions of man, the other side of this truth must now be stated. There is a profound element of changelessness, dependability, and permanence about Christ's lordship over us and His claim upon us. He is not different today from what He was yesterday, and He will not be different tomorrow from what He is today. The continuing word is also an unchanging word. But it is the written record of Scripture, the written form of the Word, that holds fast and secure the unbroken continuity with the original witness of the Word which is also a permanent witness. For the continuing Word is never in conflict with the incarnate Word, and the Christ who is our "Eternal Contemporary" is never different from the Jesus of history. "The grass withers, the flower fades; but the word of our God will stand for ever" (Is. 40:8).

This brings us yet to say that the Scriptures constitute an authoritative witness to the Word. This was one of the cardinal ideas of the Reformation: that the Bible was the authoritative guide to faith and life, that in this written witness is to be found a trustworthy, adequate, and sufficient norm by which life can be judged and faith tested. The Reformers never doubted that the Bible had a claim on them that could be equaled by no other book or collection of books. We speak of the Bible properly as a "canon of Scripture." We know that at one point in the coming of the Bible, each one of the human documents that now make up the Bible had to be selected for the canon. *Canon* meant originally a reed used as a measuring line or rule. Applied to the Bible, it means simply a collection of writings declared to be the authoritative guide for the Christian faith and life.

If we bring together everything we have been saying about the biblical witness of the Word of God—the Word of God in its written form—we will see in what way this is inescapably an authoritative witness of the Word. Being the original witness, the remembered witness, the permanent witness, it is also a witness that becomes a norm; it makes a demand; it holds a claim. To be sure, the authority of Scripture is nothing other than the authority of God himself, for ultimately all authority rests with Him. As Paul said, "There is no authority except from God" (Rom. 13:1). But God took it upon himself to reveal himself, to make himself known fully, and completely in the Man Christ Jesus. The Scriptures, being the human witnesses to that revealing work of God, derive their authority not from themselves but from that to which they bear witness. Its authority lies in its totality and its unity as a witness to Jesus Christ. Thus there can be no preaching in any truly authentic and Christian sense that is not biblical.

## Preaching and the Word - Event

In the third place, preaching the word is a part of the Word itself. One of the most fruitful studies of the nature of the Word and its proclamation is that undertaken by Karl Barth in Volume I of his *Church Dogmatics.* His concept of the threefold form of the Word has had wide influence in current theological thought.[14] While we have reversed the order which he has used and have, for the most part, used other terms, we must acknowledge our indebtedness to his own creativity. Indeed, all the way along we have been working with the threefold form of the Word. In the coming of Jesus Christ we have the disclosure of the Word or the revealed form of the Word. In the biblical records of the mighty acts of God culminating in Jesus Christ, we have the witness of the Word or the written form of the Word. And in the recital, by men to men, of the mighty acts of God, the *kerygma,* we have the proclamation of the Word or the preached form of the Word. Here we have a striking parallel to the trinitarian formula. For the three separate forms of the Word are tied together by the overarching unity and oneness of the Word.

Perhaps no modern theologian other than Karl Barth has done so much to point up this aspect of the church's proclamation as Rudolf Bultmann. I find him considerably less than convincing in the way he handles the historical ground of the *kerygma.* But in his understanding of the nature of its proclamation, he is lucid and persuasive. In Volume I of his *Theology of the New Testament,* he describes the proclamation as a "salvation occurrence," which is surely present in the "proclaiming, accosting, demanding, and promising word of preaching." Preaching is not mere reminiscence or recounting of the history, but something that continues to take place in the very proclamation of it. It is the preaching of the gospel that contemporizes the gospel. Here now are Bultmann's own words: "Consequently, in the proclamation Christ, himself, indeed God himself encounters the hearer, and the 'now' in which the preached word sounds forth is the 'now' of the eschatological occurrence itself."[15]

It is again more than a little significant that in 1907 P. T. Forsyth did not miss this important insight about the gospel and its proclamation, even when so many of his contemporaries did! For he sees preaching as something far more than the declaration of a gospel. "Nay more —far more—it is the Gospel prolonging and declaring itself."[16] "To be effective," he says further, "our preaching must be sacramental. It must be an act prolonging the Great Act, mediating it, and conveying it."[17] "A true sermon is a real deed," because, "The Gospel means something done and not simply merely declared."[18]

But we can find this as part of the emphasis of the Reformers that preaching, as Donald G. Miller puts it, ". . . is to become a part of a dynamic event wherein the living, redeeming God reproduces his act of redemption in a living encounter with men. . . ."[19] Luther said, "The preaching of the church contains in all humility our Lord's own activity." In writing to a church in the Tyrol in 1532, Anabaptist Kuentz Fuechter said, "It is my heartfelt prayer and desire for you that you be subject and obedient to the devout and faithful servants which the Lord has set over you, that you hear them diligently, and not as the word of men, but as the Word of God, for the Lord speaks through them as through instruments."[20] So the preached form of the Word is a part of the Word itself.

Now this is exceedingly high ground to take, and we will have to consider in a moment what may very well be an audacious claim that the word of man can ever become the Word of God. But the Bible itself is evidence that this has come to pass, and that according to its own witness, preaching is a part of God's total saving work on behalf of mankind, that the telling of the Christ-event is a part of the event itself.

We see this first of all in the Old Testament which is the witness of all that God has done in the history of Israel. Here, too, the witness to the action of God, the memory of it, the record of it, and the proclamation of it are so closely bound up with the divine action that it is verily a part of the action itself. The same thing is true in the New Testament where we consider more directly the action of God in the event of Christ. When we think of the event of Christ, we need to conceive of it in very broad and inclusive terms.[21] While Jesus was a thoroughly unique person in His relation to God and to man, He did not appear as the man Christ Jesus in isolation. The biblical witness is quite clear that He emerged out of a series of events or in a stream of history of which He is the center.

The event of Christ, therefore, gathers together everything about Christ, not only the background out of which He came, but also the impact of His life in the lives of men. It includes the prophecies concerning Him in the Old Testament, the facts about His being in the likeness of men *as well as the witness to* His life, teaching, death, and resurrection in the New Testament. This is to say that the proclamation of the event is bound up in the very nature of the event. The preaching of the Word is a part of the

Word itself. For this event of Christ had and continues to have such an impact on the lives of men and continues to have such a decisive power over the lives of men that they cannot but proclaim it to the world.

This is what the New Testament really is: the earliest preaching about Jesus! In the Acts of the Apostles as well as in their epistles, we see both their actions and their preaching, all growing out of their profound awareness of Christ. Moreover, it is not without significance that the books Matthew, Mark, Luke, and John are not called biographies but Gospels. In this they were well named because they are transcripts of the preaching of the apostles. The gospel was preached before it was written. Therefore, the Gospels of the New Testament are sermons, witnesses to the event of Christ, and, in a larger sense, a part of the event itself.

We cannot fully understand the meaning of God's Word and its proclamation without thinking our way back to biblical thought forms which may be very different from those of our own day. When we spoke of God's disclosure of himself in His Word, the man Christ Jesus, we observed that God acts in His speaking and He speaks in His acting. Now we are saying that the preaching of the Word is a part of the Word itself. Both of these statements can be made with the understanding that the Bible does not make as sharp a distinction between "word" and "deed" as we are inclined to make. Deeds and words must and do merge together as they did when "the Word was made flesh and dwelt among us," and as Paul expected them to do when he wrote, "You yourselves are our letter of recommendation, written on your hearts, to be known and read by all men . . ." (2 Cor. 3:2). When preaching is authentic and genuine, it is the event of Christ prolonged, extended, and reenacted. Because of what the gospel is and because of what preaching is, telling the story of the saving activity is a part of the saving activity, proclaiming the Word is a part of the Word, and preaching is bound up with what is preached.

Therefore, the sermon is more than a form of public presentation like a panel discussion, a dramatic reading, or a lecture, which may or may not be used according to inclination or "effectiveness." It is inescapably a part of the life of the church. Preaching is more than a technique of communication which can be readily exchanged for one that may prove to be more "exciting." It is part and parcel of the event which it proclaims. The pulpit is not just a platform for a man to air his views, even though they be on a religious subject. For the man who stands before a worshiping congregation, proclaiming the word that he has heard, is participating with the congregation in the Christ-event. So Karl Barth is moved to ask, "What event in the world is more momentous and decisive than Christian preaching?"[22]

### The Energy of the Spirit

Finally, preaching the Word is energized by the Holy Spirit. Here we choose our words carefully, for this is exactly the way in which Paul puts it as he thinks with gratitude of his friends at Thessalonica. "We also thank God constantly . . . that when you received the word of God which you heard from us, you accepted it not as the word of men but as what it really is, the word of God, which is at work in you believers" (1 Thess. 2:13). The word translated "work" comes from the same Greek word (*energeitai*) from which we also get our English word *energy*. In other words, the preached Word, accepted as such by the believer, is not immobile or passive within his life but active and dynamic. For it is God's Holy Spirit that suffuses the whole proclamation of the church with His power—moving, working, energizing the believer who truly hears the Word.

There is always the temptation to think of the Holy Spirit in terms that are vague, mystical, and unreal, as though we were dealing with that which does not have the solid ground of reality beneath it; or it is often imagined that the Holy Spirit has to do with a highly emotionalized state of intense feeling, although intense feeling may often be involved. And, again, the work of the Holy Spirit may be assigned exclusively to the bizarre, unexplainable happenings of life, although rational explanations may be rendered impossible.

The Holy Spirit is always closely and very deeply related to the very Jesus whom we see in the pages of the Gospels. For Jesus gave the explicit promise to send the Holy Spirit (Jn. 15:26), that He will come in the name of Jesus (Jn. 14:26), that He will teach and bring to remembrance all that Jesus said (Jn. 15:26), that He will say those things which Jesus had to say in His earthly ministry but could not because men could not bear it (Jn. 16:12), that He will guide men into all truth, but speak only what he hears, never on His own authority (Jn. 16:13). We are not surprised, therefore, when the Book of Acts tells us that Peter and John ". . . spoke the word of God with boldness," for "they were all filled with the Holy Spirit" (Acts 4:31).

Not only is the Holy Spirit always closely and deeply related to the Jesus of the Gospels. There is a similar close relation between the Holy Spirit and the Word in all of its three forms: revealed, written, and preached.

The Anabaptists gave special thought to the relationship that exists between the Word in its three forms and the Spirit. A doctoral dissertation by Walter Klaassen, dealing precisely with this relationship, is entitled significantly, *Word, Spirit, and Scripture in Early Anabaptist Thought.* Dr. Klaassen points out that among the Swiss Brethren of the sixteenth century, "The Spirit must make the Word alive, but the revelation of the heart must always be in accordance with the norm of Scripture. Only through the Spirit can the Word flourish and become alive in our hearts." The call of God, said Balthasar Hubmaier, is both an inward and outward call. "The outward drawing takes place through the public proclamation of his holy Gospel—the inner drawing is that in which God illuminated inwardly the soul of man that it understands the truth that is beyond contradiction, persuaded by the Spirit and the preached word."[23] "Man's word becomes God's word," declares Karl Barth. We can surely believe, therefore, that man's word becomes God's word because the Holy Spirit establishes it in the lips of the preacher and the ears of the hearer.[24]

It is a profoundly humbling experience to stand in this most exposed of all positions, between the Word of God and the world of men. Humanly speaking, no man can presume to speak the Word of God, no matter how virtuous or intelligent or eloquent he may be. But here precisely is a mystery which no man who has ever preached the Word has ever been able to fathom. Here exactly is an outpouring of grace for which no man has ever been worthy. Yet somehow in the wondrous ways of God, the halting, broken, and human words of men are in the Christian proclamation made the vehicles of the Word of God, and faulty, fallible, and feeble human creatures like common earthen vessels are made the bearers of the priceless treasure of the gospel. "But we have this treasure in earthen vessels," said Paul, "to show that the transcendent power belongs to God and not to us" (2 Cor. 4:7).

Thus it can be said that it is the Spirit illuminating and quickening that makes the word of Scripture a living Word. But it is the word of Scripture that gives concreteness, content, and meaning to the work of the Spirit. It is the Spirit that contemporizes and makes available to man in all ages and conditions the Word made flesh, but it is the Word made flesh that molds and shapes what the Spirit says. For as Jesus himself said, the Spirit "will not speak on his own authority" (Jn. 16:13). When the Spirit and the Word made flesh, as well as the word of Scripture, are brought together and held together, the Spirit in all ages and conditions of men will guide into all truth. So the incredible miracle takes place that the word of a fallible human creature becomes the earthen vessel for the Word of God, as the proclamation and the hearing are carried on "from faith to faith" (Rom. 1:17).

It is certainly not with any conscious intention on our part, but we are often in the unfavorable position of depreciating or cheapening the work of the Holy Spirit. In our passion for visible success we expect the Holy Spirit to produce our kind of results: those that can be measured numerically or plotted statistically. We imagine that the Spirit is subject to our manipulation, our organizational efficiency, our studied techniques, and our imaginative structures. This is no condemnation of structures or techniques, whether new or old. But there is always the temptation to claim too much for them, to assume that somehow they ignite the fires of the Spirit. Being the expert planners that we are and having mastered the know-how of advertising, publicity, crowd-getting gimmicks, group experience, and communication, we tend to leave little or nothing to the caprice of the Holy Spirit and allow no leeway for the wind that blows where it wills.[25]

The Holy Spirit has been promised; therefore, there is no need to coax or cajole Him into coming, even if we could. Furthermore, there are no forms or structures that can compel or even lure the Spirit into coming where perhaps other forms or structures might fail. The Spirit has been promised, so that all that needs to be done on man's side is to keep the human channels free and open. Like the wind that blows where it wills, so the Spirit of God is in no way subject to human limits or pressures. But in a believing faith, in prayer, "worship," Bible study, and in the preaching of the Word, the human channels are opened and kept open. For the Spirit has a relation to the Word that it does not have to any form or structure. Spirit must always stand over structure. The preaching of the Word from faith to faith opens the human channel for the Spirit and the Spirit energizes the preaching of the Word. So, preach the Word!

FOOTNOTES

1. Quoted in Kegley, *The Theology of Emil Brunner* (New York: The Macmillan Company, 1962), pp. 326 and 8.

2. Karl Barth, *Church Dogmatics,* IV, 3, Second Half (Edinburgh: T and T Clark, 1962), p. 802.

3. P. T. Forsyth, *Positive Preaching and the Modern Mind* (Grand Rapids: Wm. B. Eerdmans, 1964), p. 1.

4. Conrad Harry Massa, "Wanted: A Theology of Preaching,"

*The Pulpit* (February 1961), p. 10.

5. J. S. Stewart, *Heralds of God* (New York: Charles Scribner's Sons, 1946), pp. 68, 69.

6. Emil Brunner, *The Divine Imperative* (London: Lutterworth Press, 1964), p. 313.

7. W. E. Sangster, *The Craft of Sermon Construction* (Philadelphia: The Westminster Press, 1951), p. 195.

8. Phillips Brooks, *Lectures on Preaching* (London: H. R. Allenson, 1904), p. 5.

9. Brunner, *The Divine Imperative, op. cit.*, 312.

10. H. H. Farmer, *The Servant of the Word* (London: Nisbet and Co., Ltd., 1941), p. 56.

11. Alan Richardson, *An Introduction to the Theology of the New Testament* (London: SCM Press Ltd., 1961), p. 372.

12. H. J. Cadbury, *The Peril of Modernizing Jesus* (New York: The Macmillan Company, 1937).

13. W. M. Horton, *Our Eternal Contemporary* (New York: Harper and Brothers, 1942).

14. Dietrich Ritchl, *The Theology of Proclamation* (Richmond: John Knox Press, 1960), pp. 25 f.

15. Rudolf Bultmann, *The Theology of the New Testament,* Vol. I (New York: Charles Scribner's Sons, 1951), pp. 301, 302.

16. P. T. Forsyth, *Positive Preaching and the Modern Mind, op. cit.*, p. 3.

17. *Ibid.*, p. 57.

18. *Ibid.*, p. 14.

19. D. G. Miller, *Fire in Thy Mouth* (Nashville: Abingdon Press, 1954), p. 17.

20. Quoted by Walter Klaassen, *Word, Spirit, and Scripture in Early Anabaptist Thought, op. cit.*, p. 244.

21. John Knox, *On the Meaning of Christ* (New York: Charles Scribner's Sons, 1947), pp. 30-43.

22. Karl Barth, *The Word of God and the Word of Men* (New York: Harper and Row, Torchbooks, 1957), 123.

23. Walter Klaassen, *Word, Spirit, and Scripture in Early Anabaptist Thought, op. cit.*, p. 110.

24. Karl Barth, *The Doctrine of the Word of God* (Edinburgh: T and T Clark, 1936), p. 66.

25. *The Christian Century* (May 15, 1957), p. 614.

# 3

# The Context of Preaching

WE HAVE NOW SPOKEN OF THE CONTENT OF PREACHING which is the Word-event of God in Jesus Christ, God's speaking in His acting, His acting in His speaking, the apostolic *kerygma,* as it is witnessed to in Scripture. Out of this essential content of preaching we proceeded to formulate our concept of preaching. This way of approach is of crucial importance in view of the fact that there is a very great temptation in our day to build our concept of preaching out of materials supplied by the world instead of those supplied by divine revelation. To let the world determine what preaching is, is one thing, but to let the gospel be the determining and molding factor is quite another. On the surface, at least, this seems to place us in the position of having to decide between authenticity or relevance, which is admittedly a hard choice to make.

Let it be clear that we will address ourselves to the question of relevance before we conclude, and that the preacher needs to avail himself of whatever insights may come by way of modern techniques of communication. He must use every means at his disposal to get through to the mind and heart of modern man and do all that he can to insure his being understood. But let him remember first, last, and always that the concept of preaching is derived from the Word of God, not the world of men.

Thus, it would follow that prior to a consideration of the techniques of preaching is the theology of preaching.

The concept of preaching is shaped by the content of preaching but is executed in the context of preaching. For like any other human activity, it is not carried on in a vacuum but in a context. Since this context has characteristics all its own, it has an important bearing on what it is and on how it is understood.

### The Context of Gathering

Preaching is carried on in the context of the gathering. In the Bible the word for gathering has very special significance. You will recognize it as the word *ekklesia* of the New Testament and the word *gahal* of the Old Testament. It is nothing less than a clearly marked motif that can be traced and followed all the way through the Bible.

In the Old Testament we have it in a statement in Deuteronomy in which God commands Moses saying, "Gather the people to me, that I may let them hear my words" (4:10). In the New Testament we see it in Jesus' lament over Jerusalem, "How often would I have gathered your children together as a hen gathers her brood" (Mt. 23:37), and His well-known promise, "Where two or three are gathered in my name, there am I in the midst of them" (Mt. 18:20). We see it again in the Book of Acts, "And when they had prayed, the place in which they were gathered together was shaken; and they were all filled with the Holy Spirit and spoke the word of God with boldness" (Acts 4:31).

Along with this gathering motif, you may have noticed another that is closely associated with it. It is the hearing motif. One of the greatest preachers in Great Britain at the turn of the century was John Henry Jowett. For thirty-four years he proclaimed the gospel in a manner that was sturdy and rock-like, yet he did it with grace and beauty of utterance. In his influence he was second only to Spurgeon in England and Beecher and Brooks in America. In any case he was written about and talked about as much as any preacher in the English-speaking world at that time. One of his enthusiastic members was given to a little boasting on one occasion. To a friend who worshiped in a little chapel he said, "I hear the great Dr. Jowett every Sunday." To this the village friend made this shrewd but unexpected reply, "What a terrible responsibility!"

The Bible does, in fact, invest the hearing responsibility of man with a much greater significance than we usually give to it. As Martin Buber points out, "The Hebrew is more the ear-man, while the Greek is more the eye-man. He did not so much see God, but he did hear God's voice." The Shema, repeated daily as a confession, began with the words, "Hear, O Israel." And the prophets, like Amos for instance, made repeated use of the phrase, "Hear the Word of God." It was in this same tradition in which Jesus so clearly stood. How often were His words interspersed with phrases such as, "If any man has ears to hear, let him hear" (Mk. 4:23). And one of His best-known parables tells about four different ways of hearing the Word of God, closing with a commendation of those who "hear the word of God, accept it, and bear fruit." This is the terrible responsibility of hearing.

The gathering and hearing motifs, therefore, run alongside of each other all the way through the Bible. They come together, for example, in a passage in the Book of Acts which describes a preaching mission in which Paul was engaged in Antioch. Apart from the Jewish authorities there was an encouraging response on the part of the people, as this statement will indicate. "The next sabbath almost the whole city gathered together to hear the word of God" (Acts 13:44).

Clearly in this movement of gathering to hear the Word of God, we have not only the context of preaching but also the earliest beginnings of the church. "A Christian Church," said Dietrich Bonhoeffer, "is held together by the fact that its members are gathered around the word."[1] The radical theologians like to take off from another statement from Bonhoeffer, where he said in a letter to his godchild, "By the time you are grown up, the form of the Church will have changed beyond recognition." He did not spell out what those changes were to have been, but the fact is that he never lost sight of the centrality of the preached word in the context of the gathering. Indeed, in the same letter he said two sentences later on, ". . . the day will come when men will be called again to utter the word of God with such power as will change and renew the world."[2] "The constitution of the Church," says Karl Barth, "rests on the fact that man hears God. . . . The Church exists where this is done, even if it consists of only two or three."[3]

This is the context of preaching, the context of those gathered together who are prepared to assume the terrible responsibility of hearing. Hearing means attention. Corey Ford called attention to a very common habit that is becoming more and more widespread—that of not hearing what people are saying. "I can never finish a story," he writes, "because just as I get to the point somebody upsets a glass, or the doorbell rings, or my wife smells smoke.

Everything I say seems to remind people of something they want to say."[4] What he said with characteristic good humor is at the same time a sober reminder of the inherent difficulty which modern man has in giving enough attention so that he can actually hear what is being said. For hearing is more than registering certain impressions on man's auditory apparatus. It cannot be the casual, relaxed, and passive kind of experience we have made of it. Yet what happens in our hearing of one another happens in our hearing of the Word of God. The same preoccupation with which we approach one another, we bring to our approach to God.

To a world grown apathetic and listless and surfeited with sounds that never grow silent, there comes this urgent bid for attention. "Hear the Word of God." It is a call to disciplined and expectant listening. It implies an active human response that forcibly shuts out the noisy foreground of daily life, that silences all the clamorous and distracting noises. To hear the Word of God means to come to the gathering around the Word, not primarily to hear the fallible, human words of a preacher, but to hear God's Word through the power of the Holy Spirit coming on the vehicle of those fallible human words.

This capacity to recognize the Word of God when it is being addressed to the soul of man requires the cultivation of a personal discipline and cannot be left to chance improvisation on the one hand nor forced into predetermined structures on the other. Jesus once observed that in the course of continual following, the sheep come to know the shepherd and will not by mistake follow a stranger, "for they know his voice" (Jn. 10:4, 5). Amid the clamor of many voices, man through the careful and patient nurture of the Christian life comes to know the voice of his God which he will not mistake for any other voice. In the confused abundance of human words man can tune his ears to hear that Word which is only God's Word.

Hearing means attention and identification, but it also means obedience. In Hebrew thought, hearing and obeying are so closely related that translators have difficulty in knowing when to translate "obey" and when "hear." It is essentially the same in the Greek New Testament. This means that in the Bible, hearing implies an obedient response involving the will as well as the auditory mechanism. We cannot understand Christian obedience without realizing that it involves a prior "hearing" of the Word. Nor can one understand the full implications of hearing the Word without realizing that it must issue in an obedient response. The Greek who had an eye religion was satisfied to look at God in quiet contemplation, while the Hebrew who had an ear religion was compelled, upon hearing God's call, to answer Him in an obedient response.

Obedience in the New Testament, however, did not refer primarily to the way in which one carried out the details of a code or a law. While the moral demands of the Christian life continue to be exacting and demanding, it is ultimately not in man's own obedience, but in the obedience of Jesus that he trusts, in any case. So "by one man's obedience many will be made righteous" (Rom. 5:19). This refers specifically to Jesus' obedience to the death of the cross (Phil. 2:8). So Paul speaks very often of the "obedience of faith" (Rom. 1:5; Rom. 16:26). Obedience in the New Testament is a way of referring to the response of faith to Jesus Christ, where in Christ we participate in the obedience of Jesus, through whom we are reconciled to God. It is our decision or answer, our own act of the will in saying Yes to him that is so deeply involved in our hearing of the Word.

## The Context of Worship

Closely related to what we have just said, preaching is carried on in the context of worship. At no place is the subjectivism, about which we spoke earlier, more in evidence than in the approach we normally make to the worship of God. Worship is not, for example, a feature of human activism. Of course, worship is something we do, and we do not speak inaccurately of an act of worship. But it is God and not man who initiates worship; it is God and His mighty acts who constrains and inspires the worship of man. God calls and man answers. That is why worship must always be defined not in terms of human initiative but in terms of human response. It is the response of the human creature to the divine creator. For God's initiative is always prior to man's response, the vertical dimension before the horizontal dimension. "We love him because he first loved us."

Nor can we say that worship is conditioned by how much we say. People in our day seem to have an inordinate need to talk, to bare their souls, everywhere and always, both verbally and audibly. Granting that there is an important place for interchange on an "I"—"Thou" basis, the fact still remains that this is not worship. Worship is not an overgrown session in group therapy with a religious halo. Group therapy is excellent, but it is not worship! We are, therefore, quite wrong if we imagine that we have not worshiped until we have said something. Paul was speaking of worship when he referred to "sighs too deep for words" (Rom. 8:26). The Quakers have learned very well the use of silence as a profound expression of worship. For them silence never meant being uninvolved or being mere spectators in the act of worship. Genuineness in worship or true involvement in worship has really very little to do with the form of worship or whether we may be silent or speaking. It has, on the other hand, a great deal to do with the degree of our concentration on and openness to the being and presence of God.

It is still another misconception to hold that worship is measured by what we feel. The point is not that worship has nothing to do with how we feel or that it does not on occasion move us to very deep and intense feelings. All we are saying is that worship does not depend on our feelings; it is not determined by them, and it cannot be measured by them. Worship is not a matter of inner psychological manipulation designed to give us a heightened feeling of inspiration. It is not like standing erect, taking a deep breath, thumping your chest, and saying, "Every day in every way I'm getting better and better." Worship is a real encounter with the living God; it is the human response to the divine Creator.

Finally, worship is not directed to what we get out of it. This is to make God into a public utility, a celestial errand boy to give us what we want or think we ought to have. When we approach worship with the question, "Does worship really meet my needs?" or "What do I get out of it?" we indicate at once where our emphasis lies, and where our thoughts are centered. One may emphatically believe that worship is productive of the greatest possible results, but, as we do not get happiness by pursuing it, we do not acquire the fruits of worship by making demands on the living God.

By clearing away much of the error of subjectivism in worship, we have gone a long way to indicate what objective worship is. Consider the difference in terms of what may eventually come of worship between saying, "I don't get anything out of worship," and saying, "O Lord, Thou art very great. Thou art clothed with honor and majesty"; or between saying, "Worship doesn't meet my needs," and saying, "Let us worship and bow down, let us kneel before the Lord, our Maker! For He is our God" (Ps. 95:6, 7). What we are saying is that adoration to God for what He is in himself puts the center of worship in God and not in man.

Again, worship that avoids the perils of subjectivism is gratitude to God for what He has already done. Gratitude has always been a part of high religion and authentic worship. So while worship begins with adoration to God for what He is in himself, it moves at once to gratitude to God for what He has already done. "Bless the Lord, O my soul, and forget not all his benefits" (Ps. 103:2). Indeed, the mood of gratitude pervades the whole New Testament. Particularly is this observable in the letters of Paul. For him it was more than a little nicety, a polite courtesy to God; it was the atmosphere of his total life before God. "Giving thanks always for all things unto God and the Father in the name of our Lord Jesus Christ" (Eph. 5:20 KJV).

Finally, the kind of worship that has the mark of genuineness is an offering to God for what He is yet to do. Paul refers to this in the twelfth chapter of Romans where "spiritual worship" means the offering of our bodies (our total selves) to be acceptable to God. The point in worship is not what is acceptable to man but to God. As Kierkegaard points out, "Most Protestant church attenders act as if the church were a theater, where they were the critical audience and the minister is the actor whose act they are expected to enjoy or criticize." Paul's word translated worship (*laterian*) is the word from which we also get the word *liturgy*. (The German *Gottesdienst* seems to me to have a much richer connotation.) He is saying, "The Christian life is liturgy; and morality and cultus are one." But it would be quite wrong to conclude that Paul is thus eliminating all forms of liturgical worship. He is simply saying that living and worship cannot be separated.[5]

In "The Prayer of Consecration and Dedication" which is a part of the Communion Service in the *Minister's Manual* are the words, "and here we offer and present ourselves, in all that we have and in all that we are. . . ." That happens to be an adaptation from a prayer in the *Book of Common Prayer* which stresses the totality of our offering to God. This also means that we give every part of our worship, our service, our *Gottesdienst*. Forsyth is, therefore, quite right when he insists that preaching in Protestant worship is a part of the cultus and not a mere gratuitous adjunct to it. "The true genius of preaching," he says, is that it is "addressed to men but offered to God. . . . Further, if preaching is a main part of the Church's worship, it is a part especially of the minister's own personal worship. . . . If great art is praise, true preaching is so no less."[6]

### The Context of the Parish

Preaching is also carried on in the context of the parish. The term *parish* does not refer as it does in some countries to a geographical area. While there are some strengths in thinking of the parish geographically, the understanding here is rather that which comprises a given membership. The parish has to do with those people over whom a minister has a pastoral oversight. The parish, as we think of it, is the locus in which the minister functions as a pastor. Perhaps the best way to understand the parish as a context for preaching is to think briefly about the nature of pastoral responsibility and set down some of the more notable characteristics of the pastoral relationship.

The current contempt for preaching is equaled only by an equally vitriolic disdain for what is sometimes called parish routine or the "meetings and bleatings of the sheep." In our time of great events and world-shaking issues, everyone wants to be out where the action is—or where he thinks it is! He wants to be where new, exciting, and unusual things are happening. There is a besetting fear of being trapped by that which is dull, monotonous, and commonplace. However, the time has well passed when we need to take a second look at the matter and consider where the action really is and where it is that things are really happening. For it is very easy to be deceived and to mistake appearances for realities. Dr. John Lawson who served a village church in England during the difficult and taxing years of World War II said, ". . . he who administers small affairs of passing interest in the church stands in need of constant reminding that this apparent routine is actually the embodiment of a momentous divine purpose to sum up all things in Christ."

Reinhold Niebuhr gave a whole lifetime to a struggle for social righteousness and justice along many fronts. He started out as a minister in Detroit in the early 20's. This was the time when the labor problem was in the forefront of concern for those who were socially sensitive. But in looking back over those years, Niebuhr in later life reflected, "If I have any regret about my early ministry, it is that I was so busy being what I thought to be a prophet of righteousness, that I was not sufficiently aware of the importance of the pastoral ministry to the maimed, the halt, and the blind, in short all people who had to resign themselves to the infirmities of the flesh and who must finally face the threat of extinction."[7]

About the same time that Niebuhr went to Detroit, Ernest Fremont Tittle became the pastor of the First Methodist Church of Evanston, where he remained until his death in 1949. He, too, was a crusader for justice, a civic reformer and, in addition, an ardent pacifist. His outspoken and forthright position on many controversial issues did bring opposition and often misrepresentation. Yet whenever he was made the object of attack from those outside the church, his people stood by him, holding unequivocally to the freedom of the pulpit. But his preaching was always in the context of the parish; and when he spoke, it was not as a public oracle, but as a pastor to a people who identified themselves with him even when they may not have agreed with him.

Once when feeling against Dr. Tittle because of his particular views had become unusually intense, there was a small group in Evanston that tried to get him out of the city. Several of them came to a particular layman in the congregation to solicit his help. But he flatly refused, and in so doing made this statement: "Years ago when my wife died and my world fell to pieces and I walked all night along the lake shore, my minister without my ever asking him, walked all night beside me. He can say whatever he believes and I will listen."[8]

The parish is the context for preaching and the pastor is the one who preaches. "Who can lawfully preach?" asks a document from the Middle Ages. The answer is given: "He who has the care of souls." We need to be very sure that we know where the action really is and not miss it when we see it, or happen to be in the midst of it! Any pastor who faces with his people the fortunes and vicissitudes of life cannot be too far from the action—the real action! "Tend the flock of God that is your charge," says Peter (1 Pet. 5:2). The pastor concept is, of course, biblical all the way through. It is based on "shepherding" and finds in Jesus the chief prototype, the perfect pattern, the supreme model.

Let us now trace out some of the implications of this biblical pastor-shepherd image and see what bearing it has on the parish as the context for preaching.

The pastor is identified with a congregation. The tenth chapter of John contains one of the most complete descriptions which Jesus gives to the pastor-shepherd image. This fact he points up as being especially significant. "The sheep hear his voice, and he calls his own sheep by name." To be sure we must not press the analogy too far; we must avoid any paternalistic connotation in the pastoral relationship; and we must remember that Jesus was not thinking directly of the pastor and a congregation. And yet the early church did use the pastoral image to refer to a particular kind of ministry in the congregation. What we see in that image now is that in the pastoral relationship there is an identification, a sense of belonging, of mutual acceptance which has tremendous overtones in terms of a wholesome context for preaching. It is a relation that is built up patiently across the years, which affords not only a conducive preaching situation but an open door for pastoral service at a much deeper level.

That his preaching is rendered weak and ineffectual when as a pastor he is not deeply identified with a congregation can be illustrated by something that was reported from an issue of the Emory University *Alumnus*. A leading citizen in a community from the South and apparently a churchman gave his own view of the pastoral relationship. In writing about pastors he said:

> ". . . if their advocacy from their pulpits (in which they are, in the last analysis, the paid guest speakers) becomes sufficiently obnoxious to their listeners to cause a substantial decline in attendance and gross receipts; the clergyman mustn't be too surprised when the church fathers arrange for his transfer to more favorable climes."[9]

This is a deeply disturbing comment and one can only hope that it is not widely held. For it not only vitiates the prophetic function of the ministry by making it a pawn of the membership and converting it into a public relations post to build a successful institution, but it obliterates the pastoral function as well. For in this view the pastor is not only not a pastor in any meaningful sense of the word, but he is apparently not even a *bona fide* member of the congregation! He is a transient, an employee but not a part of the firm, a paid guest speaker with virtually no identity with the congregation.

The pastor is on a person-to-person relationship with the congregation. "I know my own and my own know me," said the good shepherd, the chief prototype of all true pastor-shepherds. Queen Victoria once complained that

Gladstone, the prime minister, always addressed her as though she were a public meeting. Well, a pastor will address the public meeting of his congregation as though they were individuals. For this is what they are! As he sees them take their places in the pew, he knows not only their names, but their struggles, their fears, their hopes, and their aspirations. And they, on the other hand, very likely know some of his. They have not only listened to him, but he has listened to them. They have not only learned from him, but he has learned from them. For before he is their pastor, he is a member of their congregation. He shares with them in their common ministry as a congregation, even though his particular function may be different from theirs.

There is no doubt that this person-to-person relationship is much harder to achieve in large congregations than in small ones. It is harder to achieve when society is mobile and the membership of the congregation is in a state of flux. And it is harder to achieve in short-term pastorates than it is in long-term pastorates. All of these factors are much more likely to prevail in our time than was the case generations ago. The struggle to maintain the person-to-person relationship with all people in a congregation will continue to be a formidable one. But this will not change the basic stance of the pastoral ministry as a context for preaching. It is a "person-minded" ministry in which the pastor is engaged, and it is as a person to persons that he preaches. His preaching in the context of the parish is shaped by the person-to-person relationship of the congregation.

Finally, the pastor cares about persons in the congregation. "The good shepherd lays down his life for the sheep." This is the true care of souls. The person-to-person relationships of the pastor with the congregation issues in his caring, and his caring deepens his person-to-person relationships. Again, as he sees them take their places in the pew, he has in a caring kind of way shared with them in the common ventures of life, the great hours, the deep hours, the difficult hours—birth, baptism, marriage, illness, old age, bereavement, and death. He has been with them in trouble and sorrow, in achievement and fulfillment. Because he cares, they have in fact struggled together. He has prayed with them and for them, and they have prayed with him and for him. This is the context for his preaching.

Preaching, even in the most unfavorable circumstances and with the greatest of ineptitude, when carried on in the context of a parish, is to a greater or lesser measure dialogue and not monologue. Moreover, the fact that it is carried on for thirty minutes without audible responses or comments from the congregation does not in itself prevent it from being dialogue. To be sure, ministers, like human beings generally, often talk too much and listen too little. It is undoubtedly an occupational hazard which requires both zeal and grace to overcome. And it is always worth all the effort that is required to make preaching assume more and more the character of dialogue. Yet it is hard to see how the preaching of a pastor who has the care of souls in the context of the parish could ever be pure monologue.[10]

Browne Barr, pastor of the First Congregational Church of Berkeley, after giving due consideration to the new and specialized forms of ministry that have been developed, reflects some disillusionment about them. It might be added that he has himself developed his share of new techniques in the work of his own parish. But he makes this observation:

> What is the role of a parish minister in revolutionary times? My contention is that his role is "to preach the gospel, administer the sacraments, and bear rule in the church." If these are times of social change, this role is all the more crucial. If the parish minister must neglect the flock committed to his care in order to exercise his own Christian citizenship, then one may wonder about his understanding of Christian citizenship.[11]

## The Context of the World

Finally, preaching is carried on in the context of the world. We will have more to say about the world in the final chapter. For in Christian preaching the Word of God is addressed to the world of men. And it is in the world that the consequences of preaching must take shape. What we have to say now about the world is only to suggest that it is another aspect of the context of preaching and one that no Christian preacher can ever dare to overlook.

The remark has recently been made that we have come to the end of a period in which theologians have rediscovered the gospel and are now in a period in which they are rediscovering the world. To this significant development in Christian thought we may, however, make two remarks. First of all, it can be said that in the wake of every new insight, or formulation of truth, or movement of thought there is always the persistent danger of exaggeration and distortion. For now as churchmen are rediscovering the world and assuming a fuller measure of responsibility for it, they are suddenly becoming vulnerable at the point of losing the gospel! The second remark is simply to raise the question regarding our alleged rediscovery of the world: When had we ever lost the world? Even Mennonites, who have been known for their strategies of withdrawal, were never as completely isolated from the world as they tried to make themselves believe.

We may properly ask ourselves whether the real burden of the church's problem in our day is that "Our church life does not intersect with the world,"[12] or whether it is, rather, that intersecting with the world, it has nothing authentically Christian to say to the world? Must we not remind the espousers of "worldly Christianity" and "holy secularism" that we have always been more worldly than Christian and more secular than holy! Surely John Howard Yoder is much more realistic and to the point when he declares, "The need is not, as some current popularizers would have it, for most Christians to get out of the church into the world. They've been in the world all the time. The trouble is that they have been of the world, too. The need is for what they do in the world because they are Christians."[13]

Harvey Cox in a conversation with Nels Ferré remarked, "Nels, you choose truth; I'll choose relevance, and we'll see who gets further by his choice."[14] Relevance is certainly the popular choice. But we may soon wonder how long the flock of God can survive the husks of relevance. For the current badge of relevance is to be able to quote knowingly from Hugh Hefner. *Time* magazine reported that one minister delivered his "talk" with a huge picture from *Playboy* magazine in the background. According to a recent quip, everyone is now wanting to assume a "worldier than thou" attitude.

This is certainly not a call to retreat into the isolation

of innocence or naivete, or to bury our heads in the sands, or to play at little games when the world around us is falling apart. This is a plea for a ministry based on biblical and theological content. At a time when the work of scholars in honest and thorough biblical research has never been more fruitful, when aids to personal Bible study have never been more readily accessible, it is nothing less than tragic that these insights find so little embodiment in our world or even in the thinking of Christians in our world.

As for relevance, Paul Scherer has this penetrating comment: ". . . to the ever-changing panorama of the years the Word of God, properly understood, never has to be made relevant. Too much honest, misguided toil has been devoted to that. The Word of God is already relevant. It was relevant before we arrived on the scene. The honest toil is called for as one seeks to understand it, and by understanding it to apprehend its relevance. All it asks is that instead of being adjusted to our modern situation, or exploited to ends it never had in mind, it be allowed to address, at this time and in this place, what is most deeply characteristic of human existence."[15]

But the Word of God is addressed to the world of men and can have no meaning to the mind of man apart from the world. For it is to man in his world that the Word is addressed, and man's being in the Word is not separated from his being in the world. And since the Word of God is not static but dynamic—an incarnate, eternal, living, continuing Word—it addresses itself concretely and specifically to those points in life, individual and collective, where moral decisions are required. The Word of God in itself is not a principle from which man is expected to make his own applications, although principles as moral guides may be deduced from the dependability and faithfulness of God's will. There is a word from God about Vietnam, about the Arab-Israeli conflict, about the race problem, about sexual morality. Therefore, the Word does not require to be made relevant; it requires only to be heard, to be obeyed, and to be done.

We have spoken of the church gathered around the Word; we must now speak of the church scattered into the world. It is not, as we have said, that we need to go into the world, for we are there already. It is rather that we must be sure that we have something to take into the world, that our being-in-Christ has no meaning if confined to the sanctuary of the church, but only as it is combined with our being-in-the-world; and that we do in the world the Word that we hear in our worship.

Here is the conclusion of the whole matter which has been put very simply by John Knox of Union: "It is not for a new metaphysic or a new science that our age dies—that its heart dries up. It is for a fresh telling and fresh believing of that ancient story. . . . The old story must be told again, told in such a fashion that men again will hear it, again will understand its meaning, again will believe its truth. For the story has not lost its ancient power, so long as man is man and the world is the world."[16]

So, "Preach the Word!"

FOOTNOTES

1. Dietrich Bonhoeffer, *The Communion of the Saints* (New York: Harper and Row, 1963), p. 155.

2. Dietrich Bonhoeffer, *Letters and Papers From Prison* (London: Collins, The Fontana Library, 1965), p. 160.

3. Karl Barth, *God in Action* (New York: Round Table Press, 1936).

4. Corey Ford, "Has Anybody Heard Me Lately?" *The Reader's Digest* (May 1955), p. 22.
5. Alan Richardson, *An Introduction to the Theology of the New Testament* (London: SCM Press Ltd., 1961), p. 300.
6. P. T. Forsyth, *Positive Preaching and the Modern Mind* (Grand Rapids: Wm. B. Eerdmans, 1964), pp. 66, 67.
7. Reinhold Niebuhr, *Applied Christianity* (New York: Meridian Books, Inc., 1960), p. 135.
8. Daniel D. Walker, *Enemy in the Pew?* (New York: Harper and Row, 1967), p. 173.
9. Franklin H. Littell, *From State Church to Pluralism* (Garden City: Doubleday and Company, Inc., Anchor Books, 1962), p. 126.
10. Franklin H. Littell, "Laymen Renew the Church," *The Mennonite* (April 20, 1965), 264.
11. Browne Barr, "Bury the Parish?" *The Christian Century* (February 15, 1967), p. 202.
12. J. Lawrence Burkholder, quoted in *The Mennonite* (August 17, 1965), p. 510.
13. Quoted in *The Christian Century* (August 23, 1967), p. 1808.
14. Nels F. S. Ferré, "Living Truth," *The Pulpit* (November 1967), 22.
15. Paul Scherer, *The Word God Sent* (New York: Harper and Row, 1965), preface, p. xi.
16. John Knox, *The Gospel, the Church and the World,* Kenneth Scott Latourette, ed. (New York: Harper and Brothers, 1946), p. 25.

# 4

# The Consequences of Preaching

The preaching transaction, when it is true to all that it was intended in the purpose of God to be, revolves around two foci: the Word of God and the world of men. It, therefore, allows that when the preacher is faithful to that to which he has been called, he stands in a middle position with God and the Word on one side and man and the world on the other, seeking through a faithful exposition of Scripture to bring about a living encounter between the two. When in the power of the Holy Spirit this takes place, preaching not only achieves its true nature but becomes a part of the word-event of God, centering in His self-disclosure in Jesus Christ. It is then itself a part of the total saving work of God on behalf of the world and all men who live in the world.

The consideration into which we are about to enter brings to its final issue that which we have to establish step by step up to this point. It is the content of preaching that shapes the concept of preaching. But it is in a clearly defined context that preaching is carried on. Now, however, it needs to be said that preaching issues in authentic consequences. It produces results. But the results that we should seek or expect to find should be only those that are in keeping with the true nature of preaching. As the content shapes the concept, so the concept actualized in the context shapes the consequence.

In view of this we should be wary of judging the consequences of preaching in the wrong way, of expecting our kind of success, or of insisting on results that may be quite secondary. Here is where so many who currently castigate the preaching ministry go wrong at the very start. They fail to see that the New Testament never did insure for preaching the kind of results that could be calculated numerically, measured statistically, or plotted on a graph. Nor can results be determined ultimately by any elaborately planned and carefully executed survey. The Holy Spirit does not seem to have our penchant for clearly measurable results!

## Words and Deeds

To look at the consequences of preaching from another point of view, consider these words from the first chapter of the Letter of James. "Let every man be quick to hear, slow to speak . . . and receive with meekness the implanted word, which is able to save your souls. But be doers of the word, and not hearers only, deceiving yourselves. For if any one is a hearer of the word and not a doer, he is like a man who observes his natural face in a mirror; for he observes himself and goes away and at once forgets what he is like. But he who . . . perseveres, being no hearer that forgets but a doer that acts, he shall be blessed in his doing" (1:19-25).

That preaching is not destined necessarily to produce

our kind of results can be seen more clearly now in the light of this passage. For here the consequence of preaching is the final link in a chain having to do primarily with the Word of God. We have considered some of these links already, but they may now be identified more closely as follows: the disclosure of the Word, the proclamation of the Word, the hearing of the Word. Now we can add another link that bears directly on the consequence of preaching. It is the doing of the Word.

This phrase may take us somewhat by surprise. We speak quite readily about preaching the Word or hearing the Word; and we speak often about believing the Word or understanding the Word. But what really does it mean to do the Word? There are several references in the writings of John to "doing the truth" (1 Jn. 1:6; Jn. 3:21). And Jesus closes the Sermon on the Mount by saying, "Every one then who hears these words of mine and does them will be like a wise man who built his house upon the rock." Whatever else it may mean to do the Word, it is clear that the Word of God is not a vague abstraction far removed from the conduct, the decision-making, as well as the vicissitudes of daily life. It touches life at every vital and essential point so that the Word of God is not only something revealed, proclaimed, and heard, but also something that must be done.

An address given before the General Assembly of the Presbyterian Church U.S.A. by the late Henry R. Luce, bore the title: "Deeds Not Words Now Needed in Race Relations."[1] The fact that it was given more than twenty years ago does not alter the point we are trying to make. It is the kind of comment that might very easily be made today and one with which it would be very hard to disagree.

For perpetual talking that never initiates action, and words that are never pressed into deeds soon become not only meaningless but virtually dishonest. However, it does need to be pointed out that this statement, like so many others of its kind, separates words and deeds in a way in which the Bible never does.

This characteristic of biblical thought may be somewhat alien to our way of thinking, but it is positively crucial if we are to understand the true consequences of preaching. For the Bible refuses to put words and deeds into alien or separate categories; inescapably they merge. This has been the basic understanding with which we have been working all the way. It came up again and again as we referred to God's mighty acts. Indeed, we see it in the two mightiest of all the mighty acts of God. We see it in His act of creation. As the writer of the Epistle to the Hebrews says, "By faith we understand that the world was created by the word of God . . ." (11:3). We see it also in His act of redemption in Christ Jesus. Here it is John who says, "And the Word became flesh and dwelt among us . . ." (Jn. 1:14). There is, then, no final separation between the words of God and the acts of God.

Let us test this further by looking at the life and ministry of Jesus. Can you say that you will take His deeds but not His words, or would you prefer His words and not His deeds? Yet how will you separate His acting from His speaking? When did He speak that He was not at the same time acting? Or when did He act that He was not also speaking? This was precisely the reason why He was eloquent and why it could be said of Him, "No man ever spoke like this man!" (Jn. 7:46).

Therefore, when man utters an authentic Word from

God it is not only a word spoken but a deed done. And when in response to the word spoken, man fashions it into a deed, it is not only a deed done but a word spoken. What is needed in race relations as well as in all the relationships of life and all the problems of moral conduct is not deeds *instead* of words. The need is rather for authentic words which, because of their very authenticity, cannot be separated from genuine deeds.

### The Doing of the Word

The proclamation of the Word must issue in the doing of the Word. This is the consequence of preaching. Fortunately, the passage in the Letter of James, true to its biblical orientation, has some rather specific indications as to what it means to do the Word. James is very clear, to begin with, that doing the Word does mean hearing the Word. All that we have said so far about hearing the Word has had to do primarily with its relation to the proclamation of the Word. What we are to say now will bear on its relation to the doing of the Word.

To conclude from this passage that doing the Word is more important than hearing the Word, or to assume that one who does the Word does not need to hear the Word is to misread the passage altogether. For if Word and deed belong together as we have said that they do in biblical thought, if the Word must shape itself into a deed in order to be relevant, and the deed must be shaped by the Word in order to be authentic, then it is of critical importance that man must know what the Word is. In the passage which puts such very great stress on doing the Word, the Apostle James does not overlook the precondition of hearing. "Let every man be quick to hear . . .

and receive with meekness the implanted word." So even now as he speaks of the peril of hearing that does not issue in doing, he recognizes what is plainly true that one cannot do a Word he has never heard.

It is quite possible to be a doer without being a doer of the Word. It is possible to be busy and active without ever having heard the Word. And it is possible to hear and do but to keep both activities in separate compartments, so that hearing does not influence doing, and doing does not result from hearing.

When Jesus was in the home of Mary and Martha, Mary sat at His feet and heard His word. But Martha, we are told, was distracted by the immediate tasks of providing the meal. Now it was not Martha's readiness to assume responsibility, her energy as a doer, or her willingness as a worker that brought upon her head the rebuke of Jesus. It was rather her distraction from the Word. Because her doing did not grow directly out of her hearing, she did, in her concern for many things, miss the one thing needful.

There is something of Martha in all of us. There is something of Martha that is typical of the church in America today. Let us be reminded at once that Martha loved Jesus; she did not mean to stand against Him; she wanted deeply to serve Him. Moreover, she knew how to shoulder responsibility with energy and drive. This is precisely the quality in American Christianity that is the utter despair of European churchmen when they see it in us. Gibson Winter is devastating in his description of it. He speaks of the trivialization of religious life, an overemphasis on activity that leads further and further into a stultifying maze of superficiality. This, he says, is the "organization church, the community of good works, the Protestant system of penance where atonement for guilt is made through organizational drudgery. It is the treadmill where men and women grind out their salvation."[2]

Overdrawn as this surely is, it nevertheless points to a tendency that we need to avoid at all costs, for it eventually leads to activism which is very different from doing the Word. The line between the two is admittedly a very fine line, but also a very crucial line to draw. For as John Knox says, "It is possible to lose one's soul in a program of highly useful activity."[3] But doing the Word, a very different thing, requires that we must again and again and again hear the Word.

Again, doing the Word means seeing yourself in the Word. As James puts it, the man who hears but does not "do" virtually deceives himself. ". . . He is like a man who observes his natural face in a mirror . . . and goes away and at once forgets what he was like." After Carl Sandburg had published his monumental series of books on the life of Abraham Lincoln, the product of a prodigious amount of work stretching over a period of twenty-two years, a friend asked him what he was going to do with himself now that this huge project was complete. He replied, "Now I must find out who this man Carl Sandburg is."[4] There is no more insistent question that ever plagues the mind of man for some kind of an answer than the question, "Who am I?" And there is no form of ignorance that brings him such misery as not knowing who he is, or knowing who he is and then forgetting it.

One September morning a father and his son were on their way to the Grand Central Station in New York City. The son was going to college for the first time, so it was a serious moment for both of them. Just before the train was about to leave, there were many things that crowded into the father's mind to say, but he confined himself to only one statement, one which the son never forgot: "Bill," he said, "never forget who you are."[5] But who was he? Who are you? Who am I?

Eugene O'Neil in his play, *The Great God Brown,* tells of a man who lay dead on the street. A policeman with a notebook and a pencil asks someone nearby, "Well, what's his name?" and the person replied, "Man." Then the policeman demands, "How do you spell it?"[6] Long, long centuries ago the psalmist asked the same question in other words, "What is man that thou art mindful of him?" (Ps. 8:4).

Abraham Lincoln was a great American and a truly great human being. But after a thorough study of his life, Sandburg felt that he had yet to answer the question: Who am I? Jesus was nothing other than the Word made flesh. After a long and careful study of his life, Albert Schweitzer could say, "There is no historical task which so reveals man's true self as the writing of a life of Jesus."[7] So it is in the mirror of the Word of God that we see ourselves as we are before God and therefore as we are really. We see what we now are as well as what we ought to be. "Man is the creature made visible in the mirror of Jesus Christ,"[8] says Karl Barth. But the man who hears the Word but does not do it, says James, is like the man who sees himself in the mirror of the Word—he sees what he is, against what he ought to be, but he does nothing about it. He does not repent, he does not pray for God's transforming power, he does not even feel an overpowering sense of unworthiness. He promptly forgets it and lives out his days in the most blinding self-deception imaginable.

Once again, doing the Word means realizing your being through the Word. One who sees himself in the Word, instead of promptly forgetting what he sees, needs not only to hear the Word but to receive it into the inner citadel of his life like a seed implanted in him. "Receive with meekness the implanted word." It is not because we are self-sufficient, or gifted, or intelligent, or even virtuous, but because of what we have seen of ourselves in the Word, that we are in any position to receive the implanted Word. In our response to the Word, we move, therefore, from the place where we see ourselves in the Word to the place where the Word can be seen in us. As Paul phrased it, "I live; yet not I, but Christ liveth in me" (Gal. 2:20 KJV). Something new, something not of himself, something infinitely greater than himself had now taken possession of him.

This is, in fact, the profoundest experience life knows anything about. For it means that the focus of life, its center of gravity, its inner support, is now in the implanted Word, in that Christ within. One who thus permits his life henceforth to be nourished, enlightened, and ruled by Him becomes a new being and participates in a transformed existence. For the implanted Word saves man's soul; he becomes what he was meant to be, and he achieves true manhood. The point we are trying to make is summarized by Emil Brunner in very forceful language. "God wants to have me—myself—for His own, and not merely my actions. In the strict sense of the word no action can be 'good;' only the agent of the action can be 'good.' "[9]

This points up another important difference between doing the Word and mere activism. Activism rests on energy, on drive, on a valiant human achievement in effort. But the whole self is not involved in it. It does not proceed from any great depth of being. But the doer of the Word, in contrast to the mere activist, is one who has the Word implanted within him, which transforms his whole existence so that all his doing proceeds from a new being. The true doer of the Word is the one who realizes his authentic being through the Word.

Finally, doing the word means controlling your conduct by the Word. The total range of man's behavior now comes under the banner of Christ because man has now realized his true being through the Word. Everything he does proceeds from that being and reflects its unmistakable character. For all of life has now come under a new control, a new constraint. Doing the Word is finally a spontaneous, unstructured, but perfectly natural expression of the Word that, just as inevitably as light is made to shine, works itself into every facet of human conduct. It permeates the whole of life with the Word from God which man has heard and to which he has responded.

Once when the devil and all his consorts were gathered together, so that story goes, it was reported that the Christians on earth were experiencing a new outpouring of the spirit which was completely transforming their behavior. This naturally brought great concern to that convocation of demonic spirits. But the prince of devils came through, as usual, with the comforting and reassuring word. "So the Christians on earth have a new experience of their faith. Be not dismayed, my friends. For you see they will not have it long. I am going to earth and help them organize it!" The ridiculous story may serve to point up a sober fact about the manner in which we are so much inclined to work. We assume that in order to do the Word, we must organize and set up a new activity and support our planned programs; and surely we cannot possibly do the Word unless we appoint a committee! It is not without reason that Gibson Winter refers to the American church as the "organization church."

This is not to say that organization does not have an important place in the functioning of a church in our modern world. We would be lost without it. But doing the Word is not a special activity, or program, or area of life. It cannot be caught in a slogan or channeled into a planned project. The winds of God's Spirit blow where they will. There are two words in the Greek New Testament which are translated "doer." The one is the word *pragmatikos* from which we derive our word *pragmatist*, and the other is the word *poietes* from which we derive our word *poet*. It is the second word that is used here. The doer of the Word is not the practical-minded pragmatist who is at heart an engineer, a planner, one who knows how to make things "succeed." The doer of the Word is rather the poet, who knows how to feel the winds of God and is profoundly moved by them. He hears the Word in the depth of his soul and in response to it he fashions it in his own life with newness and freshness. The doer of the Word is he who in all of his life and in all that he is given to do lives under the controlling, constraining power of that Word which is from God.

## The Field of the World

Many of the parables of Jesus have their setting in the out-of-doors, reflecting the common experiences of sowing and reaping. In one of these he suggests, "The seed is the word of God" (Lk. 8:11). In a closely related parable, also in an agricultural setting He says, "The field is the world" (Mt. 13:38). For it is to men living in the world that the Word of God is addressed. And it is in the world that the consequences of preaching must take shape. The Christian has no choice but to take the world seriously. Nor has he any cause to seek escape from its problems and its perils. Since the seed is the Word and the field is the world, the Word of God has meaning only in terms of the world of men. It is the locus in which the doing of the Word takes place.

One of the Uncle Remus stories tells about Brer Rabbit who had been caught by his bitter enemy Brer Fox. While Brer Fox was deciding what to do with his victim, Brer Rabbit suggested that the worst thing that he could possibly do to him was to throw him into a brier patch. But no sooner had he done this than Brer Rabbit hopped away and called out, "Bred en bawn in a brier patch, Brer Fox—bred en bawn in a brier patch."

Sometimes we think that Christianity, having fallen into a world like this, has no chance to survive, that its only hope is to keep as far away from it as possible. Yet we have only to remind ourselves that it was the world that God so loved. It was the world that Christ came to save. It was the world that God reconciled unto himself. And it was into the world that the disciples were sent. So in a world where there is every compound of evil that human wickedness can devise, the church cannot exist as a mere enclave of piety into which brands plucked from the burning are kept in safety "till the storms of life are past." If the seed is the Word and the field is the world, and if the Word of God is addressed to the world of men, then we can say that the Word was born and bred for a brier patch such as this. If the world is the field of God's redeeming activity, then we need to hear what God is saying to men in our world.

Moreover, Jesus made it clear that those who were to follow Him were to be the salt of the earth, reminding them, "If salt has lost its taste . . . It is no longer good for anything." He said that they were to be the light of the world, this time reminding them, "Nor do men light a lamp and put it under a bushel" (Mt. 5:13, 14). It is in the proclamation and hearing of the Word that saltiness is maintained. It is in the doing of the Word in the world that the light is taken out from under the bushel. Thus in the revealing, proclaiming, hearing, and doing chain of experiences the Word has both transcendence and relevance.

To separate the Word from the world in our own clumsy and faulty way is to put us into the position of being out of touch with the Word and the world. We lose the Word because we fail to apprehend its relevance to the world. We lose the world because we fail to hear the Word which is transcendent over the world. Where salt has lost its saltiness, there is nothing in us that is transcendent over the world. Where the light in us is under a bushel, that within us that may be transcendent over the world is not relevant to the world. How can we be salt to the earth, maintaining our transcendence over the world and our authenticity as Christians? At the same time, how can we be light to the world, demonstrating our relevance to the world and our mission as Christians?

This is how we are to do the Word in the world. For the world is not only the context for preaching the Word but the field for doing the Word. The consequence of preaching is to be realized not only in the lives of men but also in the world of men. And Christ, the Word made flesh, if He is Lord at all, is Lord above all. And if He is Lord above all, He is Lord over all.

### The Ministry of the Word to the World

Having gathered around the Word, we scatter into the world. After we have responded to the call to "come," we feel the compulsion to "go." It is in the world that the Word requires to be done.

First of all, doing the Word in the world is to carry on a ministry of presence. Thus we start with the simple fact that in order to be the salt of the earth, it is essential for the salt to be in the earth and not apart from it. What may seem to be too obvious even to mention or a level of beginning too low even to consider is, in fact, an exceedingly important point. Do not minimize the very basic consideration that one who is genuinely in Christ is also unequivocally in the world. He makes common cause with it; he shares in its struggles and participates in its life. He comes to grips with the world and does not seek to escape from it. While as a Christian he is not altogether of it, he is altogether in it. In His prayer for His followers, Jesus lifted up these words in supplication to God, "I do not pray that thou shouldst take them out of the world, but that thou shouldst keep them from the evil one" (Jn. 17:15). Long before the Christian says anything or does anything, he is there in the world, a part of the whole spectrum of life in the world.

The man who has truly heard the Word addressed to him in his world cannot avoid the struggles going on in the world because it is the field where God himself is working. So having heard the Word of God in worship, he is in a position to recognize the action of God in work. Because his being in Christ cannot be separated from his being in the world, he is not only a man in Christ but also a man in the world. Indeed, all the more because he is a man in Christ is he able to be human with other men and to converse with them on the basis of their common humanity. For he can be no less concerned for other men than was Jesus. This means that he is in the world to function in a provocative ministry of presence.

When Ezekiel was called to minister the Word to his own people who lived in the loathsome ghetto along the river Chebar, his resentment could hardly contain itself. One would have guessed that in such bitterness of spirit his ministry would surely fail. But then something happened to change not so much the situation as his approach to it. One rendering of the Hebrew text puts it this way, "I sat where they sat, and remained there astonished among them seven days" (Ezek. 3:15 KJV). Before he said anything at all or did anything at all, he was there with them. He felt the hurt which they felt and saw life as they had to see it. How different was the situation when he saw it from the inside and not the outside! And what was more, his resentment was gone.

Sometimes in our eagerness to witness to the world, we often forget that the Christian life means being something before it means doing something. In other words, we begin too soon—before we have anything authentically Christian to say to the world on the one hand, and before we have adequately prepared the way for true communication on the other. It is worth reminding ourselves about the way salt works in the earth—that it is doing most when it seems to be doing nothing at all. So is the ministry of presence; it is often most provocative when it is least boisterous.

Theodore Wedel tells about the response of a young officer in the British Armed Forces to a Christian appeal that had been made to him: "Don't try to help me or preach to me, or tell me what I ought to think yet. Don't work for my salvation, show me yours, show me it is possible, and the knowledge that something works will give me courage and belief in mind."[10] As the result of his years of experience in the East Harlem Protestant Parish, George Webber sharpens this point still further when he says, ". . . keep quiet until the world asks the questions."[11]

This is not to dampen the zeal for a spoken witness to the faith at a time when Christians are often far more silent than they ought to be. It does call attention, however, to the very great function of the ministry of presence in doing the Word in the world. For doing the Word means, first of all, being available to other people and being ready to listen to them wherever they are. But will the world ask the questions? We cannot but believe that the world will when doing the Word is the result of hearing the Word, when those who are in Christ exhibit His marks on their lives and reflect the unmistakable radiance of His presence. It will ask questions if it sees concrete demonstrations of what the Word says in practical demonstrations of self-forgetfulness. Then the world will ask questions, and then it becomes extremely important that, having heard the Word, we are able to give a reason for the hope that is in us.

Doing the Word in the world, however, implies a ministry to persons. God's care for the world is always with the understanding that it is because of the people who are in the world. So God's Word is not addressed to an empty world, and man's doing of the Word is always in connection with other men. For not only did God in His wisdom and power bestow on man His very own image which man in his sin defaced, but God in His love and grace bestowed on man His very Son whose perfect obedience made the image visible again. Thus, in both creation and redemption God placed upon man the seal of His love. In Paul's classic statement he says it this way, "But God shows his love for us in that while we were yet sinners Christ died for us" (Rom. 5:8).

But what Jesus demonstrated in His death He had already proclaimed in His life. He had sought in every way He could to make it abundantly clear that God's love, no less than His own, was directed toward them, and that because of it, people had worth before God. But let it be set down clearly that man's worth as a person is the result and not the cause of God's love to man. For it is not because of man's worth that God loves him; it is rather because of God's love that he has worth. The clearest evidence for this is again the fact that even "while we were yet sinners Christ died for us" (Rom. 5:8). Paul says in another place, "For the love of Christ controls us, because we are convinced that one has died for all. . . . From now on, therefore, we regard no one from a human point of view . . ." (2 Cor. 5:14, 16).

What Paul is saying is that because of God's love for persons, he is compelled to look at them, regard them, and deal with them in an entirely new way. Two things follow from this. First, this new regard for persons must be true of *all* persons. For it sees them now without any lines of demarcation, segregation, or exclusiveness. It sees them in terms of the fundamental oneness and unity of all mankind.

As we have seen, there is the oneness and unity of man in creation. Asks the prophet Malachi, "Have we not all one father?" (Mal. 2:10). There is the oneness and unity of man in the "fall." "For there is no distinction; since all have sinned" (Rom. 3:22, 23). And there is the oneness and unity of man in His redemption. And here Paul speaking of Jesus declares, "He died for all" (2 Cor. 5:15). As we see and regard persons, we must do so in the light of these facts and from God's point of view.

But this new regard for persons is not only true of all men; it is true of the whole man. As there is a oneness and unity of mankind, so there is a oneness and unity of men. For example, in biblical religion there is no sharp distinction between soul and body such as we are inclined to make. Nowhere does it hold that the body is the prison house of the soul or that it is the tomb in which the soul lies buried or that death is but the release from a body that is inherently evil. These notions are more Greek than Hebrew in orientation. So like His fathers before Him, Jesus did not separate the needs of the soul from those of the body in the sense that He ministered to the one and not to the other. He ministered always to the whole person, both body and soul.

All this has an important bearing on doing the Word in the world. For looking at men no longer from a mere human point of view, we see them now as the objects of God's love and persons for whom Christ died. We can no longer view them as means to our ends but as those whose very need is a claim on our service. To do the Word in the world is to perform uncalculating service because the love of Christ constrains us. Then, if and when the world asks questions, we can give a reason for the hope that is in us.

In Dickens' well-known *A Christmas Carol,* when Jacob Marley returns from death to warn Scrooge, his former business associate, about the way in which he was regarding other people, Scrooge says, "But you were always a good man of business." Then Marley replies, "Business! Mankind was my business. The common welfare was my business; charity, mercy, forbearance, benevolence were all my business." Doing the Word of God in the world of men is to make mankind our business, to carry on a ministry to persons, and to judge the structures of society, economic and social systems, as well as world orders and institutions, by what they do to persons.

Doing the Word in the world implies a ministry of reconciliation. In doing the Word in the world, it must be recognized that it is a world of tangled, strained, and broken relationships. There is an inherent estrangement of men from each other that operates at almost every level of man's being. Individuals, nations, races, and classes are set against each other. Barriers divide and walls separate so that, instead of peace and concord, there is hostility and conflict wherever men have to do with each other. Any newspaper will readily demonstrate the enormity of the problem. For almost every news story, whether on the local, national, or international level, is based in one way or another on the breakdown of relationships. The suggestion has been made, and in view of recent developments in space travel it is even more pointed, that men have learned to fly through the air like birds but have not learned to live on the earth like men. Indeed, the breakdown in relationships—this inherent estrangement—may yet lead man to commit the ultimate atrocity against the human race.

The estrangement of men from each other, resulting as it does in such abysmal suffering and widespread misery, is but an outward symptom of a deeper estrangement—man's estrangement from God. Man often does not recognize his own inner estrangement with the very ground of his human being. He does not recognize that he was made for God and that he is forever wrong until he is right with God. For whenever he is at war with God, he is more often than not at war with himself, with everyone and everything else. He cannot have alienation at the center of his being and peace and harmony at the circumference, or be wrong at the center and right at the circumference. It is, then, a two-sided estrangement with which we have to deal.

Paul confronted the condition of human estrangement which is so much a part of man's existence when he declared, "God was in Christ reconciling the world to himself . . . and entrusting to us the message (the word) of reconciliation" (2 Cor. 5:19). Men once reconciled to God need not, indeed they ought not, be estranged from each other. In Christ all the barriers which divide and all the walls which separate have been broken down. In Christ no man can regard another man from a human point of view, for all men are persons for whom Christ died. And because Christ is all and in all, "Here there cannot be Greek and Jew, circumcised and uncircumcised, barbarian, Scythian, slave, free man" (Col. 3:11).

The Epistle to Diognetus, written fifty years after the New Testament period, contains these words. ". . . Christians are not distinguished from the rest of mankind in country or speech or customs. For they do not live somewhere in cities of their own or use some distinctive language or practice a peculiar manner of life." "To put it briefly, what the soul is to the body, Christians are to the world. The soul is scattered through all the parts of the body, and Christians are, through all the cities of the world. The soul lives in the body, but it is not of the body; Christians also live in the world, but they are not of the world. The soul is shut up in the body, but itself holds the body together; and Christians are kept in the world as in a prison, but themselves hold the world together."[12]

Finally, doing the Word in the world implies a ministry of penetration. Much of what Jesus had to say about the way a Christian works or functions in the world He couched in the language of analogy. We have already referred to the salt of the earth and the light of the world. At this point let us introduce a third. "The kingdom of heaven is like leaven which a woman took and hid in three measures of meal, till it was all leavened" (Mt. 13:33). What is common in all of these figures is that these elements do not carry on their function with boisterous fanfare or loud noises. They work silently and almost without notice. They are inward qualities, while at the same time they produce very noticeable and unmistakable outward results. What is particularly true in the case of leaven, which according to scholars was a small quantity of dough left over from the previous baking, is that it works through the process of contagion, permeation, and penetration. Though it is small in size, the quality of leaven is nevertheless powerful enough to transform the larger mass.

It should be very clear by now that doing the Word in the world is not alone the function of the clergyman as the "man of religion." It is the responsibility of all the people of God and all who are of the body of Christ whose lot is also cast in the life of the world. Nor is it primarily the function of an ecclesiastical body functioning corporately or institutionally. It is the function of the clergyman to proclaim the Word in such a way that the layman will hear it in terms of his own life in this world, that he will know without question that it has to do with every phase of life, individual and social. There is a place for the corporate or "representative" witness of the church to the world. This is true not only in its direct impact on the power structures of society, but because the church, speaking and acting corporately, can serve as a helpful guide to individual decision-making and fortify the action the individual is called to take.

It is possible to become unduly disturbed on the ground that the church has not spoken or acted on a contemporary issue because the clergy has not spoken or acted, or because the church has not mobilized its ecclesiastical apparatus to bring pressure to bear on the structures of society. On the other hand, it is possible to take undue comfort in the fact that the church has spoken and acted simply because all of these things have been done, leaving the individual Christian with nothing more to do.

Again, while not overlooking the importance of such expressions of Christian witness and while recognizing that much more needs to be done than is being done, yet the church is most in keeping with its nature and mission when it works in another way. It is not primarily the official pronouncements of church bodies, or in the findings of study conferences, or even in what churches do in an organized way that decides the great moral issues of the day or makes the Christian faith relevant to the world. It is rather in what these activities, including the church's proclamation, may do to prepare individuals as they penetrate the total life of our world, working as leaven in the mass.

Daniel Jenkins sees in this misunderstanding of the church's primary function the danger of clericalism. He defines clericalism as "the effort to mark out and establish a world of religion which is to be distinguished from the other areas of life, where decisive power lies in the hands of a self-perpetuating corporation of religious experts." Therefore, he concludes that the church's influence on society and upon the secular organizations of society should always be indirect. It should be through individual church members who also become responsible members of secular organizations.[13] This is the ministry of penetration working as leaven in the lump.

Penetration of the life of the world with the Word that is heard from God takes place in a diversity of ways and makes use of a variety of methods. It means, of course, to do the ordinary things of life in an extraordinary way, to infuse the mind and spirit of Christ into all that one normally does in the life of the world. But it means also to express genuine creativity in seeking new ways of being aware of the world, listening to the world, and serving in the world. This is the place for experimental ministries, specialized ministries, unconventional ministries, yet never sacrificing content for novelty or faithfulness to the Word for acceptability in the world. For it is not the amount as much as the vitality of the leaven that makes the penetration of the mass possible.

## The Identity of the Preacher

The consequence of preaching is the doing of the Word in the world. We cannot leave this matter, however, without saying that in the faithful doing of the Word comes true understanding and insight. It authenticates the Word that is proclaimed and heard, which is from faith to faith. It is in the obedient response in terms, not only of decision-making, but also in the actual conduct of life that the truth of the Word is made plain. It is in doing the Word that what is proclaimed and heard in faith is confirmed and made more sure. "My teaching is not mine, but his who sent me;" said Jesus, "if any man's will is to do his will, he shall know whether the teaching is from God" (Jn. 7:16). Again he said, "If you continue in my word . . . you will know the truth" (Jn. 8:31). Knowing and understanding come from hearing and doing what is revealed and proclaimed.

Thus we close at the point at which we began: God's disclosure of himself in Jesus Christ as He is witnessed to in Scripture. This is the Word of God incarnate, living, continuing, and eternal. This is the church's proclamation, the Word-event of God, God speaking in His acting, God acting in His speaking. "To preach the Word correctly and beneficially," said Menno Simons, "is the highest and greatest command enjoined upon the preacher of Christ . . . ."[14] To this high and holy call some are set apart as servants of the Word. Some there must always be who can say, "Woe to me if I do not preach the gospel!" (1 Cor. 9:16). Paul's concern at the moment was not what would happen to the church, or to the people, or to the world, or even the gospel if he did not preach. What would happen to him! For his whole being, the entire manner of his life, and his very identity as a person were all wrapped up in his proclamation of the gospel.

To be sure, Paul never forgot that he was nothing more

than an earthen vessel, but he always remembered that in that very ordinary vessel the transcendent power of God had placed a priceless treasure (2 Cor 4:7). On behalf of those who were called to be servants of the Word, he could say, "For what we preach is not ourselves, but Jesus Christ as Lord" (2 Cor. 4:5). So there was no reason why he could not say, "I magnify my ministry" (Rom. 11:13). For he could say, "We are ambassadors for Christ, God making his appeal through us" (2 Cor. 5:20).

So preach the Word, humbly but without apology!

## FOOTNOTES

1. Henry R. Luce, "'Deeds, Not Words' Now Needed in Race Relations," *Current Religious Thought* (May 1948), p. 18.

2. Gibson Winter, *The Suburban Captivity of the Churches* (Garden City: Doubleday and Company, 1961), pp. 94-98.

3. *The Interpreter's Bible,* Vol. 8. (New York: Abingdon-Cokesbury Press, 1952), p. 197.

4. Joseph R. Sizoo, *Not Alone* (New York: The Macmillan Company, 1940), p. 74.

5. J. Wallace Hamilton, *Horns and Halos in Human Nature* (New York: Fleming H. Revell, 1954), p. 52.

6. Eugene O'Neil, *The Great God Brown,* In W. H. Durham and J. W. Dodds, British and American Plays 1830-1945 (New York: Oxford University Press, 1947), Act IV, Scene 2, p. 570.

7. Albert Schweitzer, *The Quest of the Historical Jesus* (New York: The Macmillan Company, 1957), p. 4.

8. Karl Barth, *God Here and Now* (London: Routledge and Kegan Paul, 1964), p. 163.

9. Emil Brunner, *The Divine Imperative* (London: Lutterworth Press, 1964), p. 163.

10. T. O. Wedel, *The Gospel in a Strange New World* (Philadelphia: The Westminster Press, 1963), p. 119.

11. George Webber, *The Congregation in Mission* (New York: Abingdon Press, 1964), p. 71.

12. E. J. Goodspeed, *The Apostolic Fathers, an American Translation,* "The Address to Diagnebus" 5:1 and 2, 6:2-4, 7 (New York: Harper and Brothers, 1950), pp. 278, 279.

13. Daniel Jenkins, *Beyond Religion* (Philadelphia: Westminster Press, 1962), p. 79.

14. J. C. Wenger, ed., *The Complete Writings of Menno Simons* (Scottdale: Herald Press, 1956), p. 164.